IS GOD ON OUR SIDE?

IS GOD ON OUR SIDE?

Richard Thomsen

IS GOD ON OUR SIDE?

My Side?

Your Side?

Their Side?

**Outskirts Press, Inc.
Denver, Colorado**

The opinions expressed in this manuscript are solely the opinions of the author and do not represent the opinions or thoughts of the publisher. The author has represented and warranted full ownership and/or legal right to publish all the materials in this book.

IS GOD ON OUR SIDE?
My Side? Your Side? Their Side?
All Rights Reserved.
Copyright © 2010 Richard Thomsen
V2.0

Cover Photo © 2010 JupiterImages Corporation. All rights reserved - used with permission.

This book may not be reproduced, transmitted, or stored in whole or in part by any means, including graphic, electronic, or mechanical without the express written consent of the publisher except in the case of brief quotations embodied in critical articles and reviews.

Outskirts Press, Inc.
http://www.outskirtspress.com

PB ISBN: 978-1-4327-6038-0
HB ISBN: 978-1-4327-6053-3

Library of Congress Control Number: 2010929072

Outskirts Press and the "OP" logo are trademarks belonging to Outskirts Press, Inc.

PRINTED IN THE UNITED STATES OF AMERICA

AUTHOR EXCERPTS
AND
READERS BRIEF COMMENTS

The Author

Could I in some way influence or help others to find that "wonderful" secret to a rewarding life?
-- God always seemed to be "near by" -
-- the answer was there when we least expected it.
We rejoiced in each others success and accomplishments.
-- I come back to those simple words,
"Prayer together."

Mirro Aluminum Co.

As a past officer/director; it had the best in loyal, faithful and long-time workers! It should and could have remained the largest cook ware firm in the world. Read what I feel really happened! Could this happen to your Company?

Ten Strong Lessons

With love and care, bring them up in His Ways.
Be responsive and loving parents.
God will lead if we ask Him and listen.
Prayer: daily pray together.

God sure acts in strange ways.
When Blessings Abound, give "Thanks!"
"Who you know" can often win out!
Never stop asking for His help!
Let us all "Witness for Christ"
Prayer is, has been and can be the Answer to "Real Change."

Reader Comments

Dr. Rev. Bruce Hanstedt

I recommend, without reservation, and with great enthusiasm, a careful study of this book. ----for the honesty -- insight -- as he ponders God's presence and guidance.

Rev. (Father) Gerald Foley

-- a masterful job of sharing your faith, prayer life and religious values and how all these impacted your life and that of your family. People can learn much from what you have written.

Richard H. Stolz (Business associate)

A true life story, written in the humble manner of a devout individual who enjoyed a busy life in the industrial world. His God, his wife, his children, his work and his community are interwoven --.

Mrs. Elaine Wigen (Close family friend)

Dick and Eli were a wonderful Christian couple, who lived their faith together and with others, and I relish the memories I have and the effect they had on my late husband's and my life. -- God was and is "on your side."

Cover Comment

Examining the cover, you in a pictorial way see just about everything we as humans experience in our life time. Good and "bad" things happen to us and in all of these areas! Young & old, rich and poor, even churches, businesses, societies, cities, countries, governments, worlds! In my opinion, what determines the outcome, result, or the final end, is determined by answering the question, "Is God on Our, my, your, their side?" Thank you for reading on, you may find the answer that fits! It took 85 years for me to recognize it. For that I am most thankful. I have been Blessed to be a Blessing!

TABLE OF CONTENTS

CHAPTER 1 1
   Recognition
CHAPTER 2 5
   Introduction
CHAPTER 3 13
   Born into a Christian Family
      Lesson #1 18
CHAPTER 4 19
   God presents Himself Strongly
      Lesson #2 26
CHAPTER 5 27
   War Changes My Plans: "God on Hold?"
      Lesson #3 30
CHAPTER 6 31
   "POP TO"! You're now in the Army Air Force
CHAPTER 7 35
   To "Dream Land" and Real Flying
CHAPTER 8 39
   From Small and Light to BIG and Heavy!
CHAPTER 9 43
   "Now 2 Engines! That means big Bombers"

CHAPTER 10 49
   A New Life! "May God Always Be Our Guide"
      Lesson #4 54
CHAPTER 11 57
   "Two Love Birds & The Almighty" Find a Job, "Plus."
CHAPTER 12 65
   Wisconsin to Chicago and Back, another Prayer Answered
      Lesson #5 70
CHAPTER 13 71
   Aluminum; It becomes part of our life!
CHAPTER 14 75
   Michigan here we come!
CHAPTER 15 85
   From Hot Steel Forging Back to Aluminum
CHAPTER 16 93
   Artificial Christmas Trees? Of Aluminum?
      Lesson #6 99
CHAPTER 17 101
   "Small Business Partnership" -- Another New Adventure
CHAPTER 18 107
   Not Always "What You Know" but "Who You Know"
   That Counts!
      Lesson #7 114
CHAPTER 19 115
   That Word, "Aluminum", Now Back in Our Lives!
CHAPTER 20 125
   "Blessed to Be A Blessing" Could We Be Worthy?
      Lesson #8 131
CHAPTER 21 133

Time To Stop Listening--Time to Plan and Take Charge!

CHAPTER 22 145
Promotion to General Manager of Manufacturing Engineering--"Plant Production!"

CHAPTER 23 151
Manitowoc Paper "New Vice President and Director of Mirro"

CHAPTER 24 161
Prayer Makes A Difference!

CHAPTER 25 165
"Christmas:" A time to Witness for Christ!
   Lesson #9 171

CHAPTER 26 173
"Eli the True Witness" in our Family and to others

CHAPTER 27 183
Mirro Corp. Stock Available! Fed Price Controls!

CHAPTER 28 195
Changes in Marketing/Sales; Automation the Word In Manufacturing

CHAPTER 29 207
Major Automation completed & the "Beginning of The End?"
   Lesson #10 218
   Lesson #11 218

CHAPTER 30 219
Twenty Six Years of Retirement and Still Going!

CHAPTER 31 233
"IS GOD ON OUR SIDE? MY SIDE? YOUR SIDE? THEIR SIDE?"

CHAPTER 32 237
Commentaries From My Four Pre-Readers & Friends

CHAPTER 1

Recognition

At completion of putting all this on paper and finding a publisher, came the question, "can I in some way let the reader gain some confidence that my "rambling" had some validity, not just my dream of what I had wished for. The decision was made to ask several individuals who knew me and or wife well enough, requesting they read what was written and then comment on content. Easier said than done; my life span was longer than many of those people that had that close relations. With little difficultly, four individuals were selected, all of undoubted integrity.

First, let me express my gratitude to my wonderful family! My three children are the instigator that is for sure! Years back, their requests, or I should say suggestion, was to write my autobiography. It was they and my dear wife that had the patience to live with me days on end. They were my pride and joy and still are. Thank you Louise, Nancy and Tom! To you we dedicate this book. (Mother & Dad.)

Nancy, Tom, Louise: Our "Prize"

I wish to thank all four of the friends who so willingly read my script from 8 ½ x 11 pages that came off the computer before editing. They were asked, if found it worthy after reading, would they care to comment on my "story". Their full "comments" are found in Chapter #32. Between this group and my own scrutiny, over 100 errors appeared from "no-ware"; I could never make that many mistakes, or could I? More important to me than finding "errors" was the written response from each. I am most grateful and humbled; thank you! So you know when and what part they played in my life, let me give a short review.

Not too many years after Wife and I moved into this retirement community, Felician Village of Manitowoc, WI, I met Rev. Foley (He allows my calling him Father). I have the greatest respect and admiration for Father Foley. I have heard he is retired but when you see the great work he accomplishes each day serving his Lord, Church and His people, I can't imagine what he must have accomplished when serving in past "active" years! I humbly thank you Father, your words are most appreciated and meaningful to me.

Dr Rev Bruce Hanstedt (Bruce to me) who still lives here in Manitowoc was pastor at First Lutheran Church for 22 years starting in 1971. That means he had to put up with me for many years! All "kidding" aside, Pastor Bruce was a person that had great influence in our family. He became a very close friend to our son Tom, racket ball games were often, there had to be many "aches and pains" as a result and I never recall either admitting defeat! My wife Eleanore was one of his students in the Bethel Bible study series. When I open her Bible or her Study book, the margins are filled with her "writings" that I am sure came from the lecturer, teacher and Pastor Bruce! Thank you dear friend; again I am humbled by his words in response to my request.

Richard (Dick) Stolz was one of many fine employees of the Mirro Aluminum Co. that I had the privilege of working with. You could say he was "my counterpart" in the Marketing/sales arena. He was and still is a young, influential, respected and innovative person. He and Frank Timberlake working together, reporting to the Vice

President of Marketing/Sales, were certainly the potential future officers in the company. We had only seen each other once or twice since my retirement in 1983. When I asked if he would honor me by reading my book, there was an immediate positive reply. His commentary leaves me a bit speechless! Thank you my dear friend.

Elaine Wigen and her late husband Howard were very close friends. We were part of a small husband/wife church group meeting regularly to sing gospel songs, enjoying great fellowship and of course "sweet snacks". The girls would always gather to celebrate birthdays, the passing of one more year, thus becoming very close friends. Those were wonderful times! Thank you Elaine for your willingness to add delightful memoriesto those years we all had together. After first reading your comments and experiences, I had a difficult time seeing through the wet eyes; thank you-thank you!! You have reinforced plus brought back wonderful memories!

CHAPTER 2

Introduction

After retiring from active work (wage earning), I had absolutely no intention of writing a book, let alone writing anything pertaining to my life or how I made a living. My main thoughts centered on forgetting the past and planning for the future. Keep in mind my early retirement at the age of 58 in 1983.

First, let me explain the name accidentally given to my wife Eleanore: that is "Eli". (Pronounced Ele, with long "e" ending) When we were still dating, brother, Jack, and wife approached their 1st wedding anniversary and we two "love birds" thought it clever to send them a very large traditional package containing all sorts of "paper" items and also a small separate gift and card, each sent on different days. The small gift was signed with our written names but the large box would contain a humorous card signed as **3W& 173**. Would they ever determine who those individuals were? (If you turn the **3W &173** upside-down, presto, you read ELI & ME.) A bit childish, true, but it was fun and as I recall, it took ages for them to see the light.

Back to how this book became a reality. Our three wonderful children that mother and I have always been so proud of and dearly love requested I write an autobiography. That sounded like a boring, waste of time for me to attempt in retirement! Much later the same request came from the grandchildren. It was rejected again and again as tedious and time-consuming, even when I was bored. The years have passed all too rapidly, and just last year, at the young age of 84, I spent a few hours at the local "Historical Society" office and museum. It was very interesting to relive some of the times mother and I had spent together in this friendly town, it having been our home since 1952!

This was the beginning of "listing" memories of the past, and I found it exciting! In fact, after a while, I could not stop! Each evening was consumed with recording some, and then more and more of our life experiences. It was really fun! While that excitement still remains, something new entered into play that brought to my realization a question that had been heard, discussed, and sometimes pondered throughout my life!

"IS GOD ON OUR SIDE?"

(My Side?--Your Side?--Their Side?)

I do hope and pray that as you read this "history of Mr. and Mrs. Me & Eli" you will find the answer to that question. I have! Without a doubt, I know, yes, I know for sure that "God Is On My Side" but, more important,

"WHEN?"

I hope you will read on and find that same answer! You may not see it right away but it's never too late to find it! While I have written most of these printed pages, it is almost a miracle to be able to add my "Dear Eli" experiences and cherished words to these bound pages. Through the years, she faithfully typed 3 to 6 page letters to family. Not just on holidays, birthdays, and special occasions but monthly and even weekly! (She could type as fast as I could dictate;

how do you think I got through college? Ha!) Many of these letters were saved by her younger sister, Gene, over the years 1962 to 1992, and found their way to me this year through daughter, Nancy! As you read, **her letters are identified by being printed in italics.** Needless to say, I have had a few red eyes and tears as I sorted through hundreds and hundreds of these loving pages, words, and memories. If I were to insert every word she wrote, this "story" would take several books! (There are over 640 pages of typed letters). Instead, I take the liberty to list only the dates of a letter and personally selected sentences and/or subjects---an attempt to convey Eli's beliefs and highlights of our close and wonderful years together and, as you will read, decades cemented together through the presence of our Lord and Savior, Jesus Christ.

Before going farther, I want everyone to know that I absolutely do not believe in predestination. In all of creation, we, as human beings, (not animals) were given the ability to make decisions. Much of our planning and determination of what the future holds for us depends largely on our upbringing. Certainly our parents, teachers, and associates help determine how we eventually make our plans and determine the outcome of our productive future. We are given a brain that has the ability to make right or wrong decisions, to make good or questionable friends, to choose where we go and with whom we associate.

Another comment or "finding" was constantly in my thoughts midway into my writing. The wife and I were, for sure, very busy people all the way up to our retirement years! I really marvel at all we were able to accomplish! I don't mean that in a bragging way, maybe it's just natural for many young couples. But I do know there is no way I could keep up with that pace today!

Let me cite just one example of how it happened that the "two of us" came to think and dream so much alike. Both of us were privileged to complete the "Bethel Bible" study series developed by Dr. Harley Swiggum. This is a two-year program that brings Old and New

Testament Scriptures to life! It is used in more than forty church denominations. It presented the opportunity for the two of us to experience the value of Christian upbringing and the power of prayer. If we dare call ourselves "Christians" then, with it, the expectation that we strive for perfection! We also know that "perfection" here on earth ended when sin showed its ugly head and Christ came to our aid with the Holy Spirit, helping us in our daily living, thus providing the hope of future perfection in the life hereafter.

Both of us were very active in our church; myself on the church council serving on just about every committee as chairman. I was also involved in the choir, trips, dinners, and studies. Eli was involved in the Cradle Roll, and Sunday school teaching, Prayer chain, Missionary for a day, the Christmas Program, Vacation Bible School, "Snip and Sew," Bible Studies, New Member Instruction, the list goes on and on! When not active at church, we regularly attended classes at the Vocational School. We took modern math, typing, computer programming, upholstery, engine repair, welding---most of which we did together. Speaking of doing things together, there was bicycle touring, hiking, flying, traveling, cooking; this list goes on and on also! I can't say for sure that others do not experience the same things but I wonder if all can experience the joy and real togetherness that we experienced. Whether apart or together, we seemed to thrill in each other's experiences, mainly in our prayer times. How that happened you will discover as you read of our life together

In that light, I would hope that you will find some answers or experiences that will lead you to accept in practice, a daily conversation with your Lord, Savior, and Partner. It will reward you beyond your expectations, just as it did for us! I am almost certain that our three children will be rather surprised and maybe even a bit skeptical as they read of the "inner dad" that is revealed in this writing. Mother's writings will confirm our relationship with Christ and will be very credible, as it surely exemplifies her everyday thoughts and messages. Her Christian beliefs and verbiage came out with ease and

INTRODUCTION

regularity, both in word and writings, and it always made me so happy and proud of her! At home, at church, on business trips with me, just wherever she was, there was Jesus, her "pal".

With dad it was a bit different and, for good reason. This pattern was initiated at a young age as I entered the Army. As you will read, God somehow placed me with individuals of diverse Christian beliefs, and we became very close friends. We enjoyed visiting each other's churches on Sundays, discussed our differences and similarities, and agreed to not attempt to "convert" one another. We met others whom we later agreed, were plain obnoxious in their insistent and pushy way. This turned us off. I later found that actions spoke louder than words, both in work and religion. Thus I became careful of where and when to express my feelings regarding my relationship with God; not because of being ashamed or reluctant about my faith but rather not wishing to be that person to turn them off! In my early 20s a very good friend of mine, his father a minister (all names or references omitted for fear of recognition) was turned off because of coerced attendance and performance of what parents felt he must adhere to. Just poor judgment and lack of parental love attached to their persuasion!

In my professional life, I learned similar lessons. There is nothing worse than a pushy salesman! A good salesman concentrates on substantiating and not exaggerations or fantasy. Today I find the portrayal of industry leaders in our nation disgusting, alarming and completely false. They are being called greedy, heartless, evil, undeserving and many worse names! Yes, there are those that will live up to those names but they are few and far between. I'm not saying there are no unethical business leaders. However, as a professional in my field, a manager, a vice president/director, and small business owner--all at different times---I think I fit the category that some single out as a "no good". In my many contacts and dealings with other managers of similar status, most (not all) are humble, hardworking, and religious people!

IS GOD ON OUR SIDE?

As you read my life story, it should be obvious that my childhood, plus my association with a certain wonderful mate, laid a foundation for eventual outcomes. Is and was God on my side? I will let you make that decision. All during these years of growth I was not always "righteous, holy and clean"! Looking back, there are many behaviors that I wish I had completely avoided Yes, there were times when I know God was not pleased with what, where, or actions taken! I have no desire to relive those times, they are past and, today, I'm so thankful again for moments spent in prayer. The two of us together, asking forgiveness, knowing we are being received with forgiveness! So this story is actually two life histories. When put together they produced one outcome that was not pre-determined, but rather molded into a production orchestrated by the decisions of two minds, each basically rooted in the same foundation.

"3W" is shown as a person starting as a child, rapidly becoming a man, selecting areas of interest as they presented themselves. Then, with guidance and support, I was able to achieve goals beyond expectation. My wife's story can hardly be stated in the same fashion as I have outlined my own. In contrast "173" is shown through her typewritten letters as a person devoted to her "total" family and her Maker. She always gave of herself that others may succeed. I regret that so many of her letters are "missing" from this writing. They would show her many moments of excitement, joy and thankfulness during school graduations, marriages and presentations of grandchildren. The question again can be asked, "Was God on our side?"

"IS GOD ON YOUR SIDE?"

With humility and sincerity, I invite you to read on!

"173 & 3W" (ME & ELI)

INTRODUCTION

THE BEGINNINGS

RICHARD NORMAN THOMSEN

Born June 26, 1924 (7:45 AM)
Omaha, Nebraska
    Omaha Maternity Hospital
    2204 St. Mary's Ave.
Omaha, Nebraska
Parents: Marius Christian Thomsen (age 32 at my birth)
    Clothing Store Credit Dept.
    Julia Marthena Andersen- Thomsen (age 31 at my birth) had her own millinery store, Housewife
Home address:
    3135 N. 59th St. (Benson) Omaha Nebraska
Baptism: September, 28th 1924 By: Rev. Oliver D. Baltzly
    Kountze Memorial Evangelical Lutheran Church
    Farnam St. and 26th Ave
    Omaha, Nebraska

WIFE: ELEANORE MARIE (ZAPEL) THOMSEN

Born May 7, 1926
    Chicago, Illinois
    Grant Hospital
Parents: George Carl Zapel
    Leone Ethel Klemp; 5433 Hirsch Street, Chicago
Baptism: March 31st 1929 by Rev. F.W. Otterbein
    The North Austin Ev. Lutheran Church
    Chicago, IL

◄ IS GOD ON OUR SIDE?

MARRIAGE OF RICHARD & ELEANORE

United Evangelical Lutheran Church, Oak Park, Illinois

Rev. Arthur J. Tolo; witness Jack W. & Mary S. Thomsen

CHAPTER 3

Born into a Christian Family

1924

My first home was 3135 N. 59th St. (Benson) Omaha, Nebraska. I remember only a few things there, our family moved away when I was four or five. My aunt and uncle (Mary & Art Andersen, mother's brother) lived on the same block, just south of us. I got to know their kids (Phyllis & Ward) two or three years later when my family moved back to Omaha from Colorado. I do remember the sandbox behind the single garage on 59th street. There was a willow tree next to the sandbox. One day brother, Jack, fell out of that tree and landed in the sand—completely knocked the breath out of him. I was crying

My First Home

so hard that I never gave it a thought to go get someone to help. Also, I remember the coal shoot on the north side of the house that went through the basement window, level with the cement drive. The coal would be dumped on the drive and dad would shovel it through the window. There was also a long window seat on the south side, in the dining room that looked out over the side yard, I remember Trixie, our wire-haired fox terrier, playing with her three or four small puppies-- they were sure fun and always washing my face with their tongues. (Was God on my side then? I think so; He created all things "good"--- even those little puppies!)

1928

In 1928 or early '29 the Great Depression began kicking in and Dad must have lost his job because the family left for Longmont, Colorado where Dad bought the Skaggs's food store. This apparently was a poor investment, as we moved in short order to Denver where another food store was purchased. Shortly afterward, a large chain store moved in nearby and that business failed also. Think I started school here for only a short time before we left town and moved to the mountains for the summer; we lived in a small log cabin in Meeker Park Lodge. I recall having a great time. A small cool, clear stream ran in back of the lodge---lots of chipmunks to eat out of my hand! Often Dad took me to the "two--holed" outhouse where we sat and watched the moon just before bed time. Meeker Park was near Deer Ridge and Twin Peak Mountain. The Lodge was owned and operated by the Beaver's, son named Keith who was brother, Jack's, age. They often took me along on their hikes. As a family, we were always hiking in the nearby mountains or taking rides up above the timber line and above the clouds, where snow was often encountered. I do remember Dad putting up the flag on the 4th of July, and it actually started to snow. (I reveled in God's creation of this beautiful earth at a very young age; chipmunks ate out of my hand, and I even viewed wild flowers growing out of snow banks.)

BORN INTO A CHRISTIAN FAMILY

1931

When summer came to an end (and the money ran out) the family headed back to Omaha. Mother, Jack, and Dick lived with Grandpa and Grandma Andersen while Dad drove to Chicago, looking for a job. What a miserable condition the nation was in. However, my memories of this place are very pleasant. Grandmother was warm and loving and I spent hours at her feet or in her lap listening to stories, reading books, playing store with fresh-cut fruit and make-believe selling. She was also very religious. She read Bible verses or we sang tabernacle songs. I can remember her teaching me how to pray; I'm sure they were very simple prayers but it stuck with me. (God was sure at my side in those years!) The big side-yard and fruit trees provided lots of space for doing things. Grandpa seemed to do a great diversity of things. I remember little quirky things: oatmeal each morning was dunked in a cup of milk with his spoon, the butter and sugar being placed on the hot oatmeal to melt immediately before this cooling in the milk. Today it makes sense but not then. He also liked to remove flowers from the ground and wash their roots-- mother later told me that he did have dementia. He was always sitting at the kitchen table, watching the activities in the side yard. If we did not behave to his liking we were reprimanded and told what was wrong. He was retired from the Union Pacific Railroad and he appeared very strong and strict. I sure respected him. (He never threatened me. He'd just say, "God is watching you, not just me, and He wants you to be honest and good. That way He will always be with you and help you!")

The house (4415 Spaulding Street) was on what then seemed like a very steep hill, but today it does not seem so steep. However, I do remember in the winter that the milkman had a rough time if there was ice on the street. The poor horse pulling the milk wagon was soon sitting on its rump being pushed down the hill by the heavy laden wagon. Summer ended and it was time for school. Jack was good to me-- I had to be 6 years old at the time. He held my hand, leading the way to school that seemed so far away. At the top of Grandma hill

IS GOD ON OUR SIDE?

Grand Parents Home

was a park that we often visited. Our neighbors, the Welty's, often entertained us while sitting on their back porch steps. Mr. Welty was a teacher of deaf children in Council Bluffs, Iowa; we used to call them "deaf and dumb" kids---not so today! In the basement at Grandmas, I remember putting on "stage shows". We stacked up orange crates to hold a broomstick on each end, a sheet as a curtain. We would dance to the tune of Shuffle off to Buffalo. I had a cousin name Margie; don't know what or where or to whom she belonged? I do recall her being at Grandma's house a lot. Maybe she was related to a wealthy uncle who was said to travel the world and brought "treasures" to the house. Grandma made the best Gram Bread; it was heavy and very dark but, oh, so good. I sat many times watching her pound-kneed-roll the dough. Then she popped it into the oven to produce the most delightful aroma that lasted the day. All had to sample it when still warm from the oven. I must have spent a lot of time with her in the kitchen, even remember watching the oatmeal bubble up as it cooked for what seemed like hours each day in the double-boiler. I liked to be around her because a big hug was always available. She often let us go with her to the tabernacle where the hymns she'd sung to me were repeated and I could sing along!

We played many games; hop-scotch featured eight chalk-drawn squares on the sidewalk, and you had to toss your marker into a square, hop on one foot through the rest of the squares, turn around on the last two, and return, retrieving the marker without stepping on a line. (Standing on one foot, reaching down to pick up the marker would be impossible for me today!) All eight squares had to be won first--to achieve all made you the winner. Then came hide and seek" where we'd call: "aly-aly outs in free" (whatever that meant?) Or maybe at dusk we'd play kick the can; we also made newspaper kites, then we'd compete to see who could go the highest with paper notes running up the string! (Grandma would tell me to send a note to heaven for her on that kite string, make a wish, and God would remember it in the future!)

Those early growing up years were so important. Dad and Grandpa were very loving but, in the mind of a small child, they were not only tall and muscular but they appeared to be "infallible" in what they could accomplish. They could also be quite strict in their expectations! Dad never used it, but his leather "razor strap" that seemed "yards long"(used to sharpen his razor) was referred to as the best correction tool for "bad boys". Ouch! That would be the last thing I would ever want to feel on the rear side! Consistency in discipline was their secret and I sure respected them. They balanced it by always showing a genuine interest in me... Now Mother and Grandma that was different! Lots of time with hugs and love was their gift! Looking back, I realize the early years with my parents and grandparents were inevitably a good and joyous experiences (when and if I behaved, that is). Specialists today say (I don't necessarily agree with them totally, however) a child's first eight years are often what determines their future habits.

Young people, if there is one thing I can suggest, as you bring "new life" into your early years of marriage, be consistent, loving in your discipline and spend lots of time with your children. But that's not all. Remember the Maker of all good things, our Lord and Savior who told us to "...bring them unto Me". If there was one aspect of my early years that had the most influence on my future, it was the simple fact that God was presented as someone very important. Even that simple bedtime prayer was significant: "Now I lay me down to sleep. I pray the Lord my soul to keep. If I should die before I wake, I pray the Lord my soul to take." In future days that memorized prayer was expanded to open conversation! Was God with me as a child? I am so sure He was! (Thank you dear parents and grandparents!)

Lesson #1

With love and care, bring them up in "His Ways" at an early age!

CHAPTER 4

God presents Himself Strongly

1933

In late 1933 or early 1934, Dad came to take the family to Chicago. On trips in the 1929 Chevy, I do recall sitting on the back seat floorboard to stay warm over the centered floor heater, located over the hot muffler! We lived on the second or third floor of a brick apartment building; south side of Kingston Avenue. It was during the "Century of Progress"; commonly called the World's Fair which started in 1933.It was located on the lakefront, near what is now the Museum of Science & Industry. It seemed as if all our relatives came to visit and were given tours of the Fair. Often I tagged along. I remember the shining new Burlington Zephyr railroad train on display, the Chrysler Air Flow, the Sky-Ride high up over the fairgrounds and I even recall seeing Sally-Rand with her Feather Fans. I recall little things about our home: the Oriental rugs and brass table bowl Mom and Dad purchased, which was used for years in the dining rooms to follow.

Dad was working for Firestone Tire & Rubber in some financial or accounting position. On some holiday (4th of July, I believe), Jack entered the local area parade wearing his winter Long-Johns and pulling his red wagon with me seated in it. I remember the long narrow, covered gang-ways between the tall apartment buildings. They were dark, damp and scary to me and the cement floors were hard on the knees when you ran too fast and fell. We roller skated a lot while in the Kingston apartments. That was the time when roller skates were fastened to your shoes with clamps tightened with a key. (They never failed to come loose, and at the wrong time!) The folks made some very close friends while on the south side---friends like Dave and Nan England. Their son, David Jr. (Bud) and I became good friends, spending hours with modeling clay, making model cars, people, and buildings and make-believe nothings. We moved to another apartment for just a short time. Back then, it seemed the norm to move every spring in south Chicago. Jack started high school there but only for half the year.

1935

In 1935 we moved to Elmwood Park, 80 hundred west near Grand and Harlem Avenues on the northwest side of Chicago. We lived in a brick bungalow, (56th or 65th Court, 3 or 4 blocks north of the "Circle" and one block west of the Mill's Grade school. Jack entered Stinemetz High School and graduated in 1938. I(Interesting note; Jack's future wife, Mary Gowdy, also graduated from Stinemetz.) While living here, my close friend was Bernard Freeze (Bernie) and he lived just two or three houses north. Dad helped me build a soapbox derby racer which I entered in the official Chevy Detroit races. I won only one local race but this was a great experience.

We went to church every Sunday at North Austin Lutheran. The minister was Pastor Otterbein and Mother was in the senior choir. I remember being an usher in the balcony. This was a very large congregation; each year they held a joint service in Orchestra Hall in downtown Chicago. There were four complete Sunday services each week. It was some driving distance from Elmwood Park. Each Sunday, Mom would have the roast beef cooking in the automatic timed oven, so we could sit down for lunch soon after getting home from church. It was my job to mash the spuds as soon as possible while Dad cut the meat. So, all that to say that going to church on Sunday was not an option and we were always dressed in our "best";

preceded Saturday night with a hot bath!

I must have had problems in school, because Mom transferred me to local Missouri Lutheran School, Zoar Lutheran, for the 5th grade. It was a two room school, on the second floor, directly over the church sanctuary. Kindergarten to fourth grade was in one room, fifth through eighth grades in the other. I graduated in 1938, in a gigantic class of eight. My teacher was Mr. Al Fricke in fifth through eighthgrades. I walked or rode my bike to school, which was only six or seven blocks from home. Jack and I both got our first bikes, bought used from the local Circle store. At that time, the store even offered new bikes for rent. I think it was late 1937 when we moved to 7930 Cressett Drive in Elmwood Park. This was the first home in Chicago that we actually purchased. Dad told Jack he should buy the house across the street, He could buy it for back taxes! -- This was at end of the depression, so many foreclosed homes were now very reasonable. After graduating from high school, brother Jack went to work to earn money for college. It was during this time that Jack was hit by a police car while standing on a safety island waiting for a street car. He suffered, as a result, for many years.

My four years at Zoar Lutheran had a tremendous effect upon my life. Much of this was a result of the influence of my teacher, Mr. Al Fricke. I'm very sure I was not the only one to have been guided or influenced beneficially. He took a personal interest in each student. He lived in the immediate area and his house was open to us all; we spent many an afternoon in his home singing, playing games, talking, or asking counsel or advice: you name it and he was there to help or comfort. Mom and Dad saw it too and tried to do everything possible to help him or the school. It seems to me that besides school tuition, Dad was generous in gifts to the school. Dad donated a huge, leather bound Webster's Dictionary (at least six inches thick), and when I visited the school many years later the book still stood front and center on a stand in the classroom.

Partly as a result of Al Fricke's example, I wanted to attend Concordia

Teacher's College in River Forest, Illinois. They had just started a high school, intended to prime young people for entrance into their college program. As a young high school grad, teaching or preaching in the Lutheran church school was my forward ambition-- all inspired by Mr. Fricke. (But now I am jumping ahead in my life story.) God was sure good to me and the family throughout these early years; why? Today I feel He was with my parents, guiding them for some reason. Maybe they knew the secret of talking to Him in prayer like my teacher taught us each morning before classes started.

Zoar Lutheran School

Recess at Zoar was spent in the empty lot next to and north of the two-story school building. Playing marbles was one of my talents! I carried several cloth drawstring bags to hold all my winners. (Aggies, snake-eyes, glassies, shooters and steelies). Each type of marble had its purpose.

The two school rooms were above the church proper; the basement was our recess area in rainy or snowy weather. It also was the "theater" for our yearly stage performance presented for the parents. In my last year, I played the role of a "King" Mother had made a complete outfit, trimmed with white cotton. Dad let me wear his Masonic-Lodge sword. That was a real no-no, and the Missouri Lutheran Church frowned on such organizations! The sword had to be removed before I went on stage that evening! Dad felt bad about that and made sure to apologize, I'm sure. (Was God on my side these years of youth? I think so!)

While living at 7930 Cressett Drive we had many wonderful family experiences, and as I look back I remember all the great occasions. Dad and Mom were so family-oriented and did so many things to make home the place to be, and this togetherness was so important. Jack and I took an interest in the game of pool and we frequented the pool hall. Dad found a regulation slate-top pool table in the basement of a neighbor down the block. Privately, he gave the neighbor some money; then the neighbor told us kids we could have it for only five dollars, but we had to move it home. After that, we stayed at home more and had fun with Dad and other friends. Smart move, Dad!

The basement was a place of many activities for Jack and me. We helped Dad finish it off with ceiling tile; then he partitioned off a room for Jack's chemistry work. The furnace was separated from the large section to provide for a great rec-room. We could place

2nd Home in Elmwood Park, IL

a Ping-Pong table atop the pool table; we all became quite proficient at both games. We also were given BB guns one Christmas and spent many hours at this in a long shooting range. After I received a "0 gauge" train set gift while at our home in Elmwood Park, I took a strong interest in Model Railroads, especially upon being introduced to the HO gauge, imported from Germany. I was encouraged by my parents when they allowed me to build a long table the length of the pool room. I spent many hours here putting down track, bridges, mountains, plus the building of model rail cars and buildings.

1939

In 1939, I attended high school on the Concordia College campus, River Forest Illinois It was about five miles from home; and I rode my bike or walked every day. (There was a public bus available but I very seldom used it) Mom made my lunch each day; peanut butter sandwich mostly, plus fruit. I had a room assigned to me in the dorm. (I should say two generous upperclassmen who lived in the dorm, took me under their wing, let me have a bottom drawer in a dresser where I could store gym clothes or books.) Looking back, it was a bit crude but all went well and I was not alone in that type of set up. We were the first class to start the high school program on the campus. It was fun to room with college guys! Sports were not an option; only music; I attempted the piano. Of course religious study was a required class plus German language. I had good teachers -- at least they did something that made me enjoy school; as I recall I did quite well and had good grades to show for it. All my teachers were also teaching the college classes-- math was my favorite. My best friend was Ken Bauer; he was also a "day student," meaning we lived off campus. After graduation, he was killed in military service. I have zero recollection of any other fellow-graduates in my class of 1942.

In my second year I started private piano lessons in the downtown Oak Park shopping center. A couple of miles from campus, this was once a week after classes. It was popular music, chord system; I really enjoyed it for years. To my delight, Mom (with Dad's approval,) bought the new piano that is now in my living room. My summers were spent working for the Bodine Electric Company in the factory. Dad was the Comptroller. Pay was 35 cents per hour; (think pay increased over the summers to 60 cents) those days you were paid in cash and I took a lunch bucket. Dad had left Firestone to work at Bodine Electric—I think he started as an accountant. He became quite influential in the business world and was president of Manufacturer's Association of Chicago. Sometime in the early 1940's he left Bodine at the request of the First National Bank of Chicago, and began doing consulting work for them, thus starting his new career. As companies became heavily in debt to the bank, Dad was placed in controlling positions at these companies to pay off the loans, sell the business or foreclose. This was his work till retirement at the age of 59, after which my parents moved to Arizona.

Each summer for a week, I also went to Galesburg, Illinois to visit, Bob Lutz, a friend I had made in high school. He had a model

Dick, Dad, Mom, Jack 1942

"T" Ford that we had fun making operable. I'd take my bike on the Burlington Zephyr (the train I had first seen at the World's Fair in 1934, Wow, was I ever excited!) I graduated from Concordia, class of 1942. My plans were to enroll at Concordia College the coming fall, intent on teaching in the Lutheran schools or maybe doing ministry. (God was there and pushing me a little!)

At the age of 18 you feel as if you're on top of the world! After successfully finishing high school, I think it's natural to feel temporarily "immortal". At times, temptations surround the somewhat "gullible" and, now, more independent. You are no longer considered a "child"! I have to admit, that feeling presented itself to me. Had it not been for the Christian stability and influence placed in my "make-up" since infancy, I wonder what direction my life may have taken. God had presented Himself and I was ready to let Him show me the way.

Lesson #2

Be responsive and loving parents!
Kids look up to you for help, discipline and guidance!

CHAPTER 5

War Changes My Plans: "God on Hold?"

Early 1943

"World War 2" was in the making. If I were to register at Concordia for college, it was thought I would be exempt from the draft! All my friends were enlisting in the Army after Pearl Harbor. I signed up at the University of Illinois for Electrical Engineering, thinking I may be able to enter the ROTC.

My roommate, in a private home, was senior, Phil Kessler, an engineering student. Brother Jack had roomed with him several years

Off To The U of Illinois

before. His being a senior was so helpful in teaching me the ropes on campus! Again it appeared that the Good Lord was watching over me. This large campus was overwhelming, to say the least. Our 3rd floor room in this large off-campus home was four blocks from the Engineering Buildings. Phil guided me through registration and then gave me a "Top Grade Tour" of the campus, the surrounding shopping centers, plus "student gathering" establishments. To top it off, he gave me an invitation to visit his church on Sunday. What a break for an incoming freshman! One of our stops included the "Cosmopolitan Club," the fraternity for all foreign students. They welcomed me with open arms; some time later they made me an "honorary member" and wanted me to be a frequent guest. I loved it! That same day we visited a Sorority House where Phil was a waiter at meal times; I was soon hired as well, extra income that was helpful. (Side note: after obtaining his Masters, Phil went on to be one of the engineers on the "Space Shuttle" project for NASA.) I was able to finish ½ of freshman year; (except for Chemistry) before I enlisted in the Army Signal Corp. (Often wondered how Dad and Mom felt about that!) In that semester at the university, my chemistry teacher was a student assistant and I had a very difficult time of it. I didn't see how a passing grade was possible so I dropped out of the course to prevent a failure.

In March of 1943 I reported to Scott Field, Illinois for induction. (1627th SU (RC) as Private; Army Signal Corp. I was only eighteen years old. Many in my outfit were much older, because they were being drafted. I thought it very exciting and was very receptive to the required strict discipline. As a result, I avoided KP. Lots of marching, running for miles, obstacle courses, calisthenics and physical activities was the usual routine. You ate well, slept well, and learned to never volunteer or complain!

In April, 1943, I was shipped out to Atlantic City for "basic training" (assigned to 701 Training Group, Signal Corp). All were in one of the many board walk hotels that had been taken over by the government. Being on the Atlantic coast ,"Black-out" conditions were in effect, all shades had to be pulled at night, and no lights on the boardwalk. Days were spent digging fox holes, more drilling, running, etc. We also took classes in signal work, phone use, radio, Morris code and parades. Weekends were free; and we spent much time at the "Steel Pier" where big name bands and entertainers would put on great shows -- zoot-suits & jitter-bugging were the big fads at the time, with bobby socks for the gals. I recall becoming a pretty good dancer. My bunk pals; Lloyd Whittset& Art Vittur (Both were my approximate age; we started together in Atlantic City and remained together for most of our training, till becoming officers much later.) At the end of May, 1943, we had finished training and made ready for shipping to Europe.

One weekend, shortly after arriving in Atlantic City, the three of us applied for the Army Air Force by taking a written exam. Our main reason for this was to get out of digging fox holes in the sand. While we were standing at the railroad station platform to be sent overseas with the Signal Corp, all three of us were called out of formation and told to get our gear, stand aside and wait for an officer to come and get us. The train left without us!

Sunday was usually a day off. We three friends, and sometimes others who had an interest, would attend diverse church services. Each of us happened to be of a different background; this made it possible to worship in many different denominations; Catholic, Jewish, Lutheran and Christian Scientist. For me, it proved to be most educational and a welcome opportunity to witness these "religions." I do not recall any ecumenical programs or proposals at that time, but it was very revealing to experience the difference in beliefs. (And also some very close similarities!)

Anyone who has been in military service will attest to the fact that you have little choice in selecting who you "bunk" with, where you are stationed, and what your future will bring. My being placed into a group of men that were "church going" and not of the "party going" high living individuals is a real wonder! I can't say for sure if they picked me out or vice versa, but it did happen and for that I am most thankful. We were able to have friendly, open, and in-depth conversations on Sunday, no matter what city or army base we were at! No one was trying to convert the other, but rather showing interest in comparing. God seems to work in strange ways and this young kid fresh out of high school was thrown into a group that was a real challenge to my beliefs. Looking back, it was a background that would strengthen my own faith and help me to understand others of different beliefs. Was God on hold? Not at all; He was strengthening my beliefs!

There the three of us stood at the rail station for over an hour; all we owned lay in the bag and the case at our feet. What was in store for us this time?

Lesson #3

God will lead if we ask Him and if we listen!

CHAPTER 6

"POP TO"! You're now in the Army Air Force

Mid-1943

Sometime later a voice called out "Pop to; you're now Air Cadets and expected to stand tall!" That was on June 4th, 1943. It was a little over a year before that I'd first entered the service. I had seen a new side of life, growing up in a hurry! The early training and study of Scripture paid dividends; it found my two friends and me bringing late party goers home, placing them in the shower to sober up. (God was there giving me a hand! How fortunate that I met two men with a Christian upbringing, not Lutheran, like me, but Catholic. We took turns going to each other's church on Sundays.)

The three of us were sent to Jefferson Barracks, Missouri, Army Air Force; 27th Training Group, Squad D. What a hell-hole that was! It was hot, dirty, muggy barracks, terrible so-called food to eat, and hard work at our second forced Basic Training. After the luxury of the Hotel in Jersey and what we thought was rough Basic, this really set us back and we wondered if we had made a wise move! Luckily it only lasted two weeks; on June 17th we received shipping orders. We boarded a train and headed north!

Our destination was Williamsport, Pennsylvania, where we were assigned to CTD (College Training Detachment) at Dickenson College. We were in Squad B, 331CTD, later assigned to Squad E. It was a beautiful small town with a picturesque campus that had been a church school before the war. The stay here was delightful. We studied basic theory of aircraft, how and why planes flew; weather, aircraft identification both friendly and enemy, plus flight in small J-3 Cub craft. These flights were to see if you liked flying or got airsick! (This was a first step to determine WASH-OUT). The people were so good to us; weekends the three pals (Art, Lloyd and me) were invited to a home for dinner or a picnic. (Later Eli and I visited the campus on one of our trips out East; not much had changed. It had reverted back to the original school. The people were still the same and wanted us to stay and talk.) In late September the class received shipping orders, packed up our gear, and was off to the train station. We had no idea where we were to go-- you never knew until in route to the next camp-- then the officer in charge would read off the shipping orders and announce the destination.

Nashville, Tennessee here we come! October to December 4, 1943, we were assigned to Squad D-2, Army Aviation Cadet. It was called Prep for "Preflight". This included a lot more of the same training; constant formation marching, discipline emphasized, class work on aircraft identification and phy-ed. On Dec 5th we were assigned to Gunter Field, Alabama, and placed in A1 Squad B. It appeared we were being held in limbo, waiting for some reason for our next destination. Could it be they had plenty of pilots and we were to be released from the Army Air Corp.? As usual rumors flowed freely! Early January, 1944, we made a short trip to Montgomery, Alabama. We had made it!

At last we were to begin what was called "**Preflight Training**"

Maxwell Field, Montgomery, Alabama. Assigned to Class 44I, Squad B. Yes, this was for sure. We were going to become a part of the Army Air Corp. Spirits were high! We were there from January through part of April. Yes, you guessed it: more of the same discipline, study, physical workouts and class room with night study that never seemed to end. You never dared to miss saluting an officer or shoes shined, brass sparkling, face shaved and proper uniform! Up at the crack of day, eat by the numbers, turn all corners square, "Stand up straight, cadet!" Sounds like nit-picking but you soon learned to obey orders, show respect for rank, and never question those in command; it may mean your very life someday! If you had a leader, you followed without question! By mid-April, 1944, "boys" became men of stature, filled with pride and confidence, ready for whatever was to come. While it now sounds a bit overdone, I, for one, learned the meaning of self-pride, while not questioning leadership; I learned well to respect those in command and with the proper attitude. (Preparation for the day when a young 19 to 20 year old would be given a million dollar aircraft with the lives of others in his control.)

CHAPTER 7

To "Dream Land" and Real Flying

April, 1944

By April, 1944, we were off to **Avon Park, Florida,** with the hope and desire of finally flying! This was a small "resort town" a short distance south of Orlando. Nearby was a beautiful lodge located on two small freshwater lakes and renamed "Lodwick Aviation Military Academy." The total facility was taken over for the war effort; the three-story pillar front entrance of the spacious lodge became our barracks! Wow, what a change from the usual Army bill-of-fare. Across the lake was the former casino, converted to Ground School Training facilities. It was called "The Country Club of The Air". But here began real work on what we had been training for—we had to learn respect for our aircraft and it was our challenge to master the art of flying to a degree that demanded perfection. We were told outright that not all would remain in the ranks--- at least 10% would "wash-out!" This beginning was called **Preflight Training** and the first aircraft for Cadets to learn was the **PT17(Stearmen Biplane)**--- not an easy plane to handle. It had a **radial 220 HP Continental engine, tail-dragger** with the two landing wheels close together. This made for "ground loops" resulting in wing tip repairs and possible removal from pilot training. I had a wonderful instructor named K. Chisholm. I soloed in 9 1/3 hours; had my first check ride at 23 hours (Lt L. McQuade), check ride #2 at 44 hours (Captain Gardner), final check and completed course at 65 total hours of flying.

◄ IS GOD ON OUR SIDE?

In a letter to Dad and Mom, I stated how much I admired my instructor. At our first meeting, we were told "this thing will kill you if you're not looking," In the aircraft he was a bear but on the ground away from flying, he was always finding ways to be a father to all his students. If you made a poor judgment or an incorrect move while flying, verbal "abuse" over the intercom almost burned the wires plus your legs and knees were black and blue from the control stick beating. I attribute my success to Mr. K Chisholm; a great person, a wonderful friend, a man who knew how to be strict and rough to make you remember and never forget good fundamentals of flying. My log book shows a total number of landings during training of 180, last flight on June 22, 1944. (Four days before my birthday---what a gift, I had made the first step to being a pilot for the Army)

PT-17 Biplane, 220HP

It was real fun! After good instruction, off I could go, up there all alone, practicing loops, slow rolls, snap rolls, spins and stalls, for hours until assigned time was up! This was far more exciting than the "pre-flight" marching and athletics! For a teenaged youth there was nothing more fitting for excitement and obtaining satisfaction than what I was doing! However, a setback was just around the corner.

It was here that I first faced death as a young adult. It was an experience that stayed with me for many years, one that I dreamed of and often thought was only a dream until a trip after retirement! At a reunion meeting in Florida (1984-85) of several classes of Air Cadets that trained at Avon Park, a display of pictures on a table showed one aircraft that had landed on top of another! There was my horrible "dream"! I had landed my craft just ahead of this accident, had turned my head to see what was behind me and saw this accident. The propeller at that moment decapitating the young cadet as I witnessed it! An instructor at that reunion verified the event.

(A quick step back in time.) Recall my statements about what an influence the Lutheran grade school had in my life. My parents and my teacher were "Family and Christian Rich". After entering the Army, a pattern was set. Mom or Dad sent what I remember as weekly letters; I, in turn, did my best to return short notes (Postage was free for GI's at that time.) Mother saved some of those letters that I now have. Following is an excerpt from one of those letters. I wrote: "May, 19, 1944. "Dear Mom and Dad, last Sunday I sure was thinking about you all day - your ears must have been ringing. I went to a small church in town and the minister gave a wonderful sermon. You couldn't help think of home and all, and be just a little homesick. He talked about the home and what an important part it plays in a person's life. I certainly do believe it, especially after being away from home and mixing with other people. I'm so thankful I have such a wonderful home, with such a wonderful Mother and Dad- the best in the world! I'm so glad and certainly do appreciate the fact that I was brought up in a Christian home." (I insert this note to reflect upon how my early guidance in home, church, and school has influenced me all through life, even now at the age of 85. What makes me so happy now is to see the same influence on my family up through my grandchildren. Thank you, Lord! Now on with my life story.)

CHAPTER 8

From Small and Light to BIG and Heavy!

June 1944

On June 29, 1944, I left for **Bambridge, Georgia, 2110 AAF Base Unit "Basic Training" Class 44J** The weather was very warm and sticky! My first look at the flight line was a bit scary; the aircraft looked so big and heavy! The Stearman craft in Florida were compact, fabric-covered, with a small radial engine: these monsters looked so heavy, all metal (aluminum), huge props, gear (wheels) far apart for stability, large aluminum-covered radial engine and a fuselage that looked a mile long. The plane was a **BT-13, Vultee, Low wing, Pratt & Whitney 450HP** Engine, two place Tail dragger. This plane was *big*. It had twice the horse power, shook till you thought it would fall apart, and it was loud with lots of exhaust-- Wow! How was I ever going to get close and used to this monster! It proved to be an easy task and a joy to fly! This BT-13 was very stable on the ground and in the sky. Fun galore! For the first time, I was taught to fly close to another aircraft, and I was given an introduction to "Formation Flight." This I really liked; it took concentration and trust in the aircraft in front of you--- you had to do what he did in exactly the pattern he did it! You kept your wing a few feet below and behind his wing, your wing between his wing and elevator. You kept your eyes directly on him and his motion, never any other place. The lead plane was to maintain constant throttle so you could do the same, thus reducing the chance on over-run or slipping behind. It was a great challenge but also fun. This proved to be a good sign for me, as I later was rewarded for this natural adaptation to formation flight.

BT-13 Vultee, 450HP

Another first was instrument flying while in the air. In Florida, we were introduced to instrument flight via the LINK trainer. This was a simulator (enclosed cockpit, fastened to electric motors and mount that moved the unit similar to that in flight). You sat in this device, completely covered so you could not see anything but the flight instruments in front of you. The instructor sat at a desk with a mouse that walked on the table top, pen marking your path on a map, showing how you were flying and where you were going. Everything was recorded. It was a great tool in that day. Now, in this rather stable BT-13 aircraft, we could experience the real instrument flight.

Instrument introduction led us to night flight. Another first! What a thrill to fly at night among the stars-moon-city lights---taking off into blackness with no reference to the ground. Again, instrument training was needed. You begin to see how important the different training procedures were and why you had been taught, early on, the discipline and trust in others. You had to believe in those things wholeheartedly. I ate it up!!

FROM SMALL AND LIGHT TO BIG AND HEAVY!

My instructor was 1st Lieutenant Lee Lester, O-804183; again I had a wonderful teacher! Still wonder how I was so fortunate; seemed I always had the best-- maybe because I so liked what I was doing and they sensed that? They all seemed so friendly and willing to help! I soloed after nine hours of dual flight. Total hours flown in the craft was 76.2 hours, 146 landings, plus 10 hours in the Link trainer. My last flight in Basic and the BT13 took place on September 2nd, 1944. Up to this point my hope was to become a fighter pilot but I knew that my height probably slotted me into the larger multi-engine aircraft. Either way, I was thankful to have progressed to this stage, accepting whatever might be my fortune.

CHAPTER 9

"Now 2 Engines! That means big Bombers"

Sept. 1944

Next stop was **Freeman Field, Seymour, Indiana**, and now **"Advance Training"** September, 1944. This was the final step before receiving a status of Army pilot and officer! It was obvious to me at this point that my destination was heavy bomber bound. The flight line was filled with twin engine aircraft. Ok, I had to make the best of it; on the plus side was that after the war there could be commercial airline possibilities. The aircraft was the AT10 Twin Beechcraft, Lycoming radial engines, 295 HP each engine, 198mph, retract gear, mainly wood construction, 2 place, low wing, single rudder. It proved to be rather easy to fly and very stable. I started flying the AT10 in September, 1944, and finished January 25, 1945, a total of 96 hours with another 58 hours co-pilot time as I helped instruct Cadets in formation flight from the right seat. (For non-fliers, First Pilot (Pilot in Command) is **always** is in the left seat of the craft; copilot is in the right seat.) Night flying, again, was fun and frequent, 29 hours. Link Trainer for instrument instruction was 34 hours. Actual "under the hood" instrument time in an aircraft was 53 hours. On November 22, 1944, I passed and received my "White Card" instrument rating. Upon completion I was commissioned 2nd Lieutenant, Class 44J. It was a great feeling to have completed the training; all three of us pals who had started together were successful. Now the question was what aircraft would be our final home for overseas duty? At this point I was just happy to progress this far! We must have been one of the last classes to train at Freeman Field. As I recall, a bulletin was posted asking for volunteers to fly AT10 craft to Florida. It sounded like the Indiana field would be closed. You learned early on that it was not smart to volunteer for anything when in the Army! Instead, I was shipped out to Transition Training.

AT-10 Twin Beechcraft 600HP

Dad & Son, Both Army Pilots

Mother with Son Cadet

Son is Now a 2nd Lt

1945

In early February, 1945, reported to **Smyrna Air Base,** Smyrna, Tennessee (Near Nashville) Massive **B24s,** 4-engine bombers, lined the field everywhere you looked. The large craft was to be my next challenge! We seemed to be delayed and had free time. I took the opportunity (which I later found was frowned upon and not allowed) to find a small airport where I could get checked out in J3 Cub, solo, and then I applied for a CAA Commercial Air License. B24 flying began on Feb. 23, 1945. I found the B24 an easy aircraft to adjust to. While very large and taking a lot of muscle to fly, I found it responsive with sufficient power. The Pratt & Whitney engines seemed to take any kind of punishment you could subject it to. By the end of July, 1945, I had 137 hours of bomber flight time.

B-24 Liberator, 4800HP

My parents came to visit me on a weekend; they stayed in town but, on the Friday night when they arrived, parked their car at the far end of the runway where I happened to be flying that night. Of course, I had no idea they were there. I was practicing night landings and take-offs, what they called "touch and go"---no complete stop, just slow down and then take off again. I have no idea how many landings and take offs I did during the four or more hours of this. When it was over for the night, the ground crew informed me that their assignment was to replace the tires for the next day's flight crew! We had burned up a full set of tires in one night! They said that was normal.

"NOW 2 ENGINES! THAT MEANS BIG BOMBERS"

I was assigned a co-pilot, Lieutenant Tigert; he had served a tour in Europe for twenty flights and returned to the States, requesting assignment to B24s as co-pilot for more duty out of Italy. Everyone called him TIGER! Could he fly that B24! He taught me a lot of tricks with dos and don'ts. He had to be close to 30 years old, heavy smoker, and on the ground, very, very nervous! In the air he was right at home, calm as could be. We would play a game on the landing in which I could push his cap over his eyes on final descent, and see how close he could come to landing without seeing! Of course I, the other pilot, was ready to take over, but it was amazing how close he could come to perfect without seeing anything but the instruments! We all wondered about our future at this time. Here it was July. VE day was long past (May 8th, 2 months earlier) would we be sent to the South Pacific in B24s? The answer was soon coming!

Mid-July '45: Orders came for me to report to **Maxwell Field, Montgomery,** Alabama, **B29 Super Fortress:** Transition Training! South Pacific, here I come. I was about to fly the largest bomber ever built! Again I was so excited and pleased to have this opportunity; the very fact that I was sure to be soon headed for flights over Japan

B-29 Superfort, 8800HP

never entered my mind! All I could think of was flying this beautiful new aircraft! On August 6, 1945, I was flying in the B29, unaware that "Little Boy" was being dropped from the B29 Enola Gay on Hiroshima! Three days later, August 9th, the" Fat Man" A bomb #2 was dropped on Nagasaki as I flew. August 14 was VJ Day, the end of WW2! To my surprise we did continue our flight training until there were contrary orders issued from higher up. We flew many cross country missions, mainly via Arizona and New Mexico.

By early September, '45, training was stopped and we were sent to Gunter **Field, Montgomery** Alabama Gunter was now a single engine training base equipped with AT 6 Retract gear aircraft. I was checked out and allowed to continue flying for 14 hours, until word came for us to receive discharge or enlist for duty! I was happy the War was over and that I could return home! I was sent back to Maxwell Field where I received my discharge from the U. S. Army Air Force.

AT-6 North American, 600 HP

CHAPTER 10

A New Life! "May God Always Be Our Guide"

July, 1945

A new life for me was ahead. The young teenager that left home and school was now grown up, had seen much of life in a different world, and was now a bit bewildered. The abrupt change left me mentally unprepared. What was I to do now? Brother Jack was now married and administrated his own engineering business located in downtown Chicago. I loved drafting at school and Jack was very generous to take me into the business. I lived at home with the parents in Elmwood Park. After work I would attend school at Northwestern University, Chicago campus. I now took the chemistry which had caused me to drop out of the University of Illinois years earlier..

The eighteen months following exit from Army service are so many blanks in my memory. I see only a kaleidoscope of clashing images: times with my cousins Robert Ryder, Paul Ryder, and Midge Thomsen and life with my parents on separate occasions. During this time I was invited to Jack and Mary's apartment in Oak Park for dinner and a blind date with Mary's maid of honor---Eleanore M. Zapel. It was the beginning of a long relationship. Was God on my side? I now often wonder if He was; could it be that He was pleased with me and made so many good things happen or placed them in my path? I very much doubt that He allowed temptations to run rampant as a wide open field around me and no one to restrict where I went and what I did. So why is it, I seemed to always be in the right place, doing what turned out to be the "best" thing at the right time? Conclusion: "Upbringing", that Christian home, parents, friends, and discipline.

"Discipline" is an important word. Christian living requires discipline; sure, as Christians we believe that forgiveness is always available, no matter what the degree of wrongdoing! Yet to be "that Christian" there is a certain expectation required of us; that discipline to choose rightly! My time in the Air Force strengthened that instinct for discipline and it made me a better person, I'm sure.

At the time, I was dating several other gals. Charlene Rathfuss (lived a block from the parents) and Bea Bohm was a daughter of my parent's church friends. However, it seemed but a short time before I met Eleanore's family. During the winter of '46 I do recall many evenings spent at her home. Parking was difficult as she lived on a dead end street (Major Ave., Austin, Illinois). Snow plowing was impossible near the city, so deep ruts resulted. I could get to her house which was at the end of the block, but getting out late at night was often a challenge. She worked in the Loop, just across from Jack's office. She was also attending University of Northwestern night school so it was a natural for the two of us to have dinner and walk to campus. Many dates later I asked for her hand in marriage to which she gave me the wonderful answer of "yes". Early on, I had given Eleanore the nickname of "Eli", pronounced "Ele" with a long ending "ee")

1947

In those days, finding an apartment was nearly impossible, the war had put a stop to any new home construction so there was a terrible shortage of living space. In the summer of 1947, we found an apartment. The living room was also our bedroom; the bed would fold into the wall during the day to provide a little breathing space.. A small bath room and small kitchen faced the backyard. The place was a short distance off of Lake Street near the El tracks on the Northwest side of town. With only short notice to both sets of parents, we announced our wedding plans. On August 9, 1947 we were married at United Lutheran Church in River Forrest, Illinois, the church Eleanore and I had been attending for some time; the church where my parents had attended for several years. Pastor Hegee played an important part in our lives in the years to come. We both felt as though he was speaking directly to us each Sunday in his messages. When we met with him in our pre-marriage counseling, he made one rather simple but lasting suggestion. "Each evening, try the simple act of kneeling together at the bedside, praying together, asking forgiveness, requesting guidance and help, along with thanksgiving." Wow! After the wedding, a reception was held in her backyard; the house was filled and what a wonderful day we had! Wedding night was spent at the Drake Hotel, Chicago. The following day we drove to Milwaukee to catch the Car Ferry across Lake Michigan to Ludington. Dad was very generous to let us use their car. We spent the week in the Upper Peninsula with several trips to Mackinac Island.

When dating we both spoke together of our strong belief in Christ and desire to keep our future strongly based around a Christian home. Inside Eli's wedding band, we had the following letters engraved; **"MGABOG". (May God Always Be Our Guide)** To support this and do as Pastor suggested, each evening we learned to pray together, with many requests for forgiveness, guidance, praise and thanks. It kept us close for over 58 years. Even in her last hours, when not capable of forming sentences, she would say "thank you" after a prayer. Yes, God was on our side and kept us close for over 58 years!

Eli had a wonderful job (and boss) and with the GI Bill, I continued my college education at the University of Illinois, Chicago campus, on the Navy Pier in Chicago. I finished my second year (engineering) in Chicago, and in 1948 enrolled at the Champaign-Urbana campus.

1948

We found a second floor apartment in Urbana in which we shared the bath with the elderly landlady. We had a bed room, living room (former bedroom) and another bedroom made into a kitchen (no water). My Mother had purchased a new gas range, so we took the old one with us and I hooked it up to the gas light pipe that had been left in the wall. Furniture was sparse; lawn chairs and card tables were the thing! Our campus was quite typical; there were many newlyweds after the war---an evening's entertainment was cards (Canasta) with popcorn and soda! We had a great time and I was so happy to be back at school! Eli found work as secretary to a professor. When in Chicago we had the opportunity to buy a used 1938 Olds that seemed to be in good condition. Thanks to Eli's brother (Russ) who owned a similar model and was very capable of repairing autos, we had a good running car. Our closest friends were Paul and Lou Sistec there on campus. Together we would have a real evening out and go to the midget auto races there in Urbana fair grounds. One weekend Eli's brother Russ came to visit us from Chicago, bringing his lovely girlfriend, Helen. We spent a day at the Arlington Estate near the campus.

My major was Mechanical Engineering; plus a minor in Accounting with the hopes of going on for a Masters in M.E. Eli was such a wonderful help in my getting through college! She could type as fast as I could dictate; as a result, my written reports and essays were a snap! Back in 1942 when first coming to the University of Illinois, college seemed difficult--my interest not really in it. The war was a big distraction and I really did not concentrate much on classroom work. Time in the Army Air Force, working with Jack, getting married, all added to a much changed attitude toward school. Now there was a desire to learn as much as possible and a vision to plan for what may come in the future. Add to this the competition of fellow GI classmates who were there for the same reasons, kept me on my toes to stay ahead. Having Eli at my side was the most significant encouragement of all! We did everything together; even cooking and baking (and praying).

In the middle of my junior year an unexpected challenge came our way. One afternoon after class as I walked into our kitchen, and there stood Eli, leaning over the ironing board. She appeared as though looking for something on the floor on the other side! There was no answer to my usual greeting; when I leaned down to give her a "peck" on the cheek, I could see her eyes were shut and hands grasping the ironing board very tightly! Why she had not fallen is a miracle! After getting her to bed, I called the doctor, who came almost immediately (In those days house calls were very common). After a short time in the hospital, the news was anything but encouraging! Take your choice: Polio or Rheumatic Fever! (Again, at that time they did not know the difference, and Polio was still an unknown except for a few cases in an iron lung.) With calls to our parents it was quickly ruled that Eli would be well taken care of at mother Zapel's home; what a blessing! The car was made ready by converting the back seat to a bed and off we drove for Chicago! Once there Dr. Burdic gave a complete exam followed by strict instructions Eli was to remain in bed for many months, no strenuous activities, no walking, and no excitement. She even had to take meals in bed. What a blow! Thank goodness for Mother Zapel!

During the following year, weekends were spent driving to and from Major Avenue in Chicago. Homework in hand and a car loaded with students, luggage, and snacks. The passengers helped pay for car expenses. (tires, clutch, brakes, fuel, oil, exhaust valves, springs, muffler -----on and on). Thanks to brother-in-law, Russ, who spent hours on his back teaching me the art of auto repairs, the cost was kept to a minimum! As a result, crucial time was spent with my dear Eli where she made out my weekly shopping lists, how to cook and

IS GOD ON OUR SIDE?

bake and save, and all the rest! She also continued to type my reports as I dictated. What a trooper, she never complained and Mom and Dad Zapel were so willing to accept the cost-time-responsibility. With no activity on her part and the wonderful meals at home, her weight increased far beyond her wishes. (It exceeded my weight which didn't make it any easier for me to carry her to the bathtub. Ouch!)

Time flew that year; when the time was up, Eli's health was sound and there was absolutely no damage to her heart. Thank you, Dr. Burdic and Zapel parents, for your good advice and care. Our trip back in the trusty 1938 Olds with the back seat bed in place was a happy day. Eli recovered rapidly; the home planner, scheduler, and boss kept me busy, and school was now fun again. The thought of graduation looked very real. With money now at a premium, the plan of a Master's degree was forgotten. Instead, we explored a plan to achieve a professional engineer rating. I could take (and did pass) the written exam prior to graduation in Mechanical Engineering. (To achieve the professional engineer rating, years of actual experience had to be to gained, which came much later.) I did complete my minor in Accounting, which was very beneficial in future years.

Let me again state the importance of early youth training, example-setting, and knowledge of Christian living! With Eli's equal participation and background, we bolstered each other through thoughts and prayers that never let us down. We determined to think positive, walking forward with confidence in God's leading Hand. He sure led us through our first big test and trial! (Thank you, Lord!)

Lesson #4

Prayer! Priests, Pastors, in your marriage counseling, suggest daily prayers together, All three of them--- wife, husband and God!

"Plump" Eli and Graduate, 1950

CHAPTER 11

"Two Love Birds & The Almighty"
Find a Job, "Plus."

1950

In the last semester at campus, a new reality set in. Come graduation in February, the G.I. Bill pay would come to an end! With Eli not working, gross income would shrink to zero! With the wonderful help and talent of Eli, 60 copies of "R.N.T. résumés" were completed but only after us, together, paged through the "industrial directories" throughout the entire nation. We picked companies that caught our interest and, most important, cities and states we would like to live in. Keep in mind, there were hundreds of engineers graduating and looking for work from thousands of campuses in the U.S. Of the 60 letters, a grand total of three interviews materialized. Wonderful! But could one really be for "real"? This meant traveling, time and money. Parents were always there to help out, and this was no exception.

One of the interviews was in Chicago. That proved to be no problem; Eli's home was there. The second was in some little town in Wisconsin, north of Milwaukee, called Kohler. My parents had moved to Kenosha, Wisconsin. Kohler was not too far north from there! With these two interviews completed, we could only return to reality, busy with final exams, thinking positive and hoping for the best. It was only days (that seemed like an eternity) before we received positive offers from both! Now, which one? Our big decision had to be made!

The Kohler Company offered the best opportunity and pay. My job description was plant engineer. We loved the area and it was within easy driving distance to both parents! With little hesitation, off went our acceptance pronto! How thankful we were, and best of all, the offered salary was $3,000 per year. (At that time, top starting wage for graduating engineers was that amount, how happy we became!) Kohler, little known to us newlyweds, was certainly a common name to our elders! They were makers of the best in plumbing ware, known throughout the world and well respected. I think our parents were as pleased as we were! To top it all off for us, Kohler invited me to live at their American Club; a very large living quarters built in earlier years for employees, primarily immigrants coming from the old country to work in the factory. It proved to be a wonderful and beautiful place to start, providing an easy location to explore for an apartment in the town of Kohler as well as the nearby city of Sheboygan, Wisconsin, (with population over 40,000).

1950

The big event of graduation in February of 1950 went off without a hitch, thank goodness! It was exciting to be finished with the books, but the future challenge made it pale in comparison and we could hardly wait to explore our new life together with the unknowns that presented themselves in Wisconsin! Where would we eventually live? Could we find new friends in this strange area? Would I be accepted well by the other workers at Kohler? What is it like to find your own way in life? What kind of church would we find in such a small city? (Being from Chicago we sure had to be careful of using that term in the future!) The American Club served excellent meals at very reasonable prices---plus, they had bowling lanes and lounge areas. My roommate was Dan Whealand from Michigan; new grad plant engineer like me; both starting at the same time. Eli would have to stay with her parents again until I could find a place to call home. Weekends would bring Eli to town as we examined prospective apartments searched out during the week.

We found a very clean and furnished apartment on N 8th Street, Sheboygan. It was a few blocks from the downtown area, shopping close by, city park, lakefront just five blocks East with a small zoo, beach and grass park. It was on the second floor with three other apartments; a dentist office and a drugstore operated below. There was a garage in the rear with a small yard separating the two buildings. We couldn't have asked for anything better to start with. The month apart was not to our liking; anything at that point would probably have looked good but we did luck out with such a great place.

Kohler! It proved to be the most rewarding, educational, learning and ground breaking experience for a newly graduated so-called engineer! We had prayed for guidance in our selection of companies to work for and as I look back over our years of life together, the Lord sure led us time and time again! Here was my first job as a bread winner--being placed in an engineering department with at least 35 to 40 engineers with all areas of responsibilities: Electrical, Architectural, Ceramics, Machine Design, Product Development, Power Generation, Hydraulics, Heating & Ventilating, Transportation, Conveying-----. You name it; Kohler had it, did it, and practiced all areas of engineering. When a new factory or addition was to be built, engineers were there to design as general contractors. This was an amazing operation to witness and to be a part of.

To really top it off for me, nearly all my colleagues were college grads with many years of experience, all with great pride in their work and so willing to help us new engineers to take over for them, to learn from them, to answer any and all questions. Many were near

Kohler Co. My First "Job"

Sheboygan Apartment; Louise is Born!

retirement and they made me feel at home, as though a son! In short order they had me doing things of major importance and cost. For example I was commissioned to design a large machine to be placed in a conveyor line to automatically drill the drain holes, bottom and end of a cast iron bath tub. It was to rotate the unit 180 degrees, turn it over, complete the drilling operations, and continue its position for next operation that of accepting the next tub weighing hundreds of pounds. (This was 58 years ago!) Not too long ago I returned to take a tour of the plants with friends; to my amazement the conveyor and "my" machine were still there in operation. What a great place for me to learn! What great people I had as teachers of real engineering! You did it all, from basic design for strength, gears, motors, reduction drives, controls, hydraulics, limits, drills, switches, lubrication, safety, codes, material orders, construction oversight building in the on-site machine shop, work with purchasing and suppliers, installation oversight on the shop floor, instruction for operators---the whole ball of wax. This was to be just one of many tasks. Many times I learned the hard way, but seasoned and friendly "old hand" engineers all around me were always there to help, encourage and support me. What a wonderful way to begin my career; experience that paid dividends in the years ahead. These were individuals that would play a part in my future.

In 1950, Kohler was in the process of designing a new foundry with automated sand handling, casting and electric smelting. The complete new project was first built in miniature, ¼ inch equaling 1 foot. This model was amazingly complete in detail; it was used for critiquing purposes by all engineers and shop personnel for possible revisions and improvements. (I wonder if that could happen or be possible today.) Again, what a terrific education for me! Listening to peers and shop workers can really pay off.! The person in charge of the engineering was Elmer Gielow, just a great person in my book. After being there for some time, a shop foreman stopped me one day and asked if I had seen Jim Kohler in the last few minutes? Me, see a Mr. Kohler! He had to be kidding, I didn't know any Kohlers! Just then, the Jim I had been working with in the ceramic casting area for weeks came down the hallway. Yes, to my embarrassment it was the Mr. Jim Kohler. As I apologized, Jim quickly answered "So what, we have a job to do and I think you can sure help me!" (He was a graduate ceramic engineer, with a Master's degree) As you will read later, there were others (like Les Kuplic) that played a role in my work history.

At home, it was all good news too! After a complete exam at the local clinic, Eli announced we were to be parents! On August 31, 1950 our daughter, Louise Alice, entered our world; Miss Dr. Duckering, who lived in the apartment next to ours, only required a knock on the wall early that morning. Then, off we all went to the hospital. A wonderful person, Duckering was trained in the East and brought new procedures to hospitals in the Midwest. (Examples; Husbands in the delivery rooms; newborn with the mother the second day.)

While in pre-natal care, Eli met Annie Konz. Annie was a devout Catholic Christian and she became a very close and dear friend! She and Eli would spend hours together with baby carriages (and, later, strollers), visiting all places in town that would have them. Husband, Larry Knoz, and I hit it off well too. We spent many enjoyable evenings and weekends together. Larry ran a small wood cheese-box factory in the city of Howard's Grove, just a few miles northwest of Sheboygan. It presented a glimpse into the world of operating a successful small business; this would serve me well in the future. (A sidelight: Another new "baby" was added to our family in the month of August! The faithful Oldsmobile was not receiving the loving care shown to it earlier by brother-in-law, Russ; it had to be replaced, and we bought a gold colored brand new 1950 2 door Pontiac! We were riding in real style!)

When first in town, we visited different churches each Sunday morning. Not knowing anyone, it was interesting to see what type of greeting we did or did not receive at each church. Eventually, we selected the Methodist Church, located about six blocks from our apartment, near the lake front park and the pastor (and his messages)

"TWO LOVE BIRDS & THE ALMIGHTY" FIND A JOB, "PLUS."

made us feel right at home. It was a wonderful match and so very friendly. (Thank you again, dear Lord!) We had together (the three of us: two "love birds" and the Almighty) found a job, a wonderful worship center, a home, and Christian friends!

In our short period of married life we had experienced the reality of positive and negative things which can happen in life. Being a Christian cannot guarantee that only "good" things will come your way! The experience of Eli with rheumatic fever is an example! As humans on this earth we never know what is just around the next corner: good - bad- or neither! The question for us to answer is are we ready? I don't for a minute think that God made all this happen "just for us". However, He made it possible for us to "find our way" by being ready to accept or reject opportunities. Our daily prayers certainly helped us to recognize and be ready for whatever came.

CHAPTER 12

Wisconsin to Chicago and Back, another Prayer Answered

1951

During the fall of 1951 a troublesome situation developed at Kohler that was new and difficult for me to understand. The new foundry was partially in operation. I spent lots of time in the factory and knew many of the workers as a result. I began to notice a lack of conversation and it appeared more and more as though they (the shop workers) were avoiding me. Being a greenhorn in the world of industry, the term "labor unions" was not familiar to me or even in my vocabulary. I soon was informed as to its meaning and some background on its history at the Kohler Company! The change I was experiencing was due to the simple fact that "labor union contract" negotiations were beginning. Difficult to understand at the time, "management versus worker" relations became rather frigid. I was briefed by fellow engineers regarding the history of past serious and devastating work stoppages (strikes). To me, the people (all of them, including office-engineers-shop workers, etc.) at Kohler and the Company itself were the best. Just to be part of it was wonderful. I can only say good things about the company and the employees I had made so many great fiends and they were so good to me. However, the condition, as stated before, was troublesome and it raised questions as to what our future would look like. By early

IS GOD ON OUR SIDE?

1951 some of the new automated lines were not operating properly; the amount of rejected products was increasing, the scrap pile was growing. When studies were made regarding the problems, it always came up: "human interference." Investigators found things like a wrench left in the gear box or wires cut in a control box.

It was a very hard decision to make, but with Eli's help, we began searching the want ads for possible new work. In October of 1951 we picked up stakes and headed back to Chicago! Industrial engineer was my new title at the Webcor Company; one of the leading manufacturers of industrial and household equipment, like record players and tape recorders. Would it surprise you to hear that the plant was only a block away from the Zapel home! Yes, we were back living with Eli's parents! This time three of us! Mother and Dad were unbelievably good to us. The plan was to stay just a short time while we looked for a place to call our home. The temporary arrangement turned into four months! They were so tolerant and kind to us, we sure enjoyed being with them and it was evident the baby grandchild around the house pleased them too.

Webcor! This proved to a very disappointing adventure. Nothing but paper-paper- and more paper-with the shuffling of more paper! I did determine one thing for sure: my four years of engineering school was not needed for this sort of work and was not what I had in mind to do for a living. It did, however, teach me the importance of good record-keeping (process sheets; listing all materials, operations and routings plus time required to complete the product.) It became the backbone of standard costs used to determine margins and production efficiency. This did broaden my experience for things to come, plus it brought out meaning to the accounting minor studied at college. Not all was lost for time spent at Webcor!

Just before Christmas weekend, we received a phone call from Mr. Vern Hansen, the assistant to Elmer Gielow, the person in charge of Kohler Engineering! Unknown to me, he, too, had left Kohler to become chief engineer at a company just north of Sheboygan. I had worked with Vern extensively and we had good relations while at Kohler. What a surprise when he asked if we would be interested in moving back to Wisconsin! He wished me to consider working with him. The company was planning to start an engineering department. He suggested my driving up to interview with the president of the company over the Christmas holiday! Could this be for real?

When we made the move back to the big city of Chicago, several reasons were predominant. We missed family, plus we liked the idea of being located where so much more was available, be it entertainment, shopping, or culture. In addition, this was where we were brought up and lived all our past years! Those so-called advantages were soon removed from our minds after only a few months of the crowded streets, close set, cookie-cutter houses with the nearest park an hour's drive away. No, now we missed the quiet and open lands of the "small" town!

After only a few minutes of conversation with Eli, my return call to Vern was a question. Yes, we would like to meet and see if it would be something that had potential for our future, but how should we arrange the meeting? The person I was to meet was Mr. John Torrison, President of the Aluminum Specialty Company located in Manitowoc, Wisconsin. Their product was aluminum cookware. The city was just 30 miles north of Kohler and located on Lake Michigan. This seemed too good to be true! The meeting would be at his home; I could also visit the plant with Vern Hansen before the interview. With daughter, Louise, so young, it was agreed I would travel alone. We both were so excited to think we could return to an area we so enjoyed and a place close to our dear friends, Annie and Larry Konz!

1952

After Christmas I went to Mr. Torrison's lovely home. I was already interested due to a tour of the factory in the afternoon. I had also heard from Vern what the job would entail and what the salary with benefits would be. Mr. Torrison was a friendly person; he put me at ease right away. He appeared young and vibrant, with several children in 4th or 5th grade. It was a morning meeting. After introduction to his wife, Mary, we proceeded to the basement lounge. I was invited to sit on the plush bar stool as he proceeded to mix some unknown drink in a rather large shaker. He remarked, "How about a refreshing martini to start the day and our conversation?" (A martini? What is that! I had heard of it in service, knew it was "booze" and after too many, it was always my job to take the "friend" to base and put him in a shower, then the bed!)

"No thank you, Mr. Torrison," I replied, "liquor does not agree with me, especially in the morning." With a laugh, he poured himself a hefty glass. The usual conversation followed regarding my family, education, past work, etc. His ability to have conversation was amazing considering the amount of alcohol he was consuming! (Over the following years I learned his tolerance for and ability to handle liquor very well). To my surprise, Mr. Torrison was a member of the 1st Lutheran Church in town, plus he served on the board of regents at Luther College in Iowa. I don't recall the meeting lasting more than an hour; his final words were: "Dick, from now on just call me John. You will make a fine addition to our team. When can you join us?" Wow, I was impressed. "As soon as I can terminate all obligations in Chicago," I said. "I am confident you will see me in January." With a handshake to seal the deal, I was on cloud nine driving home to give the great news to Eli.

Before leaving Manitowoc, I made a visit to the downtown Hotel (no Motel was listed in the phone book) and also picked up the local newspaper for the "for rent" listings. At the time we felt concerned, a little worried, yet very thankful. As I look back, everything happened as though we were charmed! Mr. Torrison mentioned the company would pay for moving so we would not have to face an unplanned expense, since they were requesting me to change jobs. (That was good news; now we could find unfurnished living quarters, and purchase furnishings in Chicago where new outlet stores were just becoming popular.) Both parents listed all sorts of items they were happy to give us from their collection.

January 28, 1952 was my first day of work back in Wisconsin! Living in the Hotel was not the best, but, again, happy days were only weeks away. The builder/owners of a newly built home on the south side of Manitowoc found them in a bind over meeting house payments. If they could find a likeable couple, they felt comfortable renting the home out. We became that lucky couple! The rooms were sparsely furnished, but to be in a new home was delightful! It had one bedroom on the first floor, living-dining room, large kitchen, small bath, and an empty, clean basement. However the second floor was not even framed out. The owners became good friends; their parents were our soon-to-be neighbors and friends. As spring approached, it was fun for us to get the lawn seeded and some rooms painted. We even finished some wood trim and put it in place (helping Dad as a youth in Elmwood Park came in handy).

New Rented Home; Nancy is Born!

◄ IS GOD ON OUR SIDE?

Aluminum Specialty Co., Manitowoc, WI

One evening as we were unpacking the many boxes and still sitting on crates, we had company at the front door! It was two gents from the First Lutheran Church on N. 8th Street! Ervin Mellberg and Bob Berkedal. They were most welcome. They were there to welcome us to town, hoping we would find a church to our liking. We made it a point to visit "First" the very next Sunday; it became our church during all our years here in Manitowoc. (Our prayers had requested guidance; an answer "rang our doorbell" that evening!)

Lesson #5

"God sure acts in strange ways!" Even ringing door bells!

CHAPTER 13

Aluminum; It becomes part of our life!

1952

Work at "Specialty" was very rewarding and interesting. My job involved plant, product, packaging and industrial engineering. Both of my past positions had groomed me for this! The office and shop people were just wonderful and loyal. Work ethics were outstanding and most employees were second and third generation at the Specialty. The engineering department was rather new. Several tool and die men had gained drafting experience and learned the trade by working in the machine shop making the tools. These individuals were outstanding. (They knew all there was to know at this time about working aluminum!) This was new to me---another opportunity to learn---they were patient with me. My role was centered on plant operation, layout, equipment and control. Industrial engineering was included, which entailed establishing production rates. Specialty had two plant locations: the main office and factory in Manitowoc, and a second plant located approximately 28 miles west in Chilton, Wisconsin.

How was it that all but one major manufacture of aluminum cooking utensils was located in Wisconsin? Manitowoc had two companies: Aluminum Specialty and Mirro Aluminum; Metal Ware in Two Rivers, Layse Aluminum, Kewaunee; West Bend Aluminum, West Bend: and Regal Ware, in Kewaskum. Wear Ever was out east and a division of Alcoa Aluminum. When first introducing the new "light metal", Alcoa looked for places to produce its growing output. Wear Ever was started out east. The founders of Aluminum Goods which became "Mirro" were approached by Alcoa to manufacture novelty items and cooking utensils in this part of the country. Over the years, tool and die men left Mirro and formed the new companies throughout the state of Wisconsin.

The first major project undertaken in my new adventure was to be in the industrial engineering area. Mr. Torrison introduced us to individuals from the Lochrum-Evans consulting firm out of Racine, Wisconsin. Mr. Lochrum had developed a technical method to replace time studies, used in establishing production standards. Time study was initiated by use of a stop watch, which determined and established "production piece rates". A piece rate, simply put, is: "a standard time allotted for an operator to produce "x" number of the product (piece) assigned". This was performed by a time study person when the product was first made. This person timed and rated the operator as to efficiency. This standard time not only rated performance of the worker but was also used to predict the "standard" labor cost of the product produced. (Added to this was related material cost, allotted indirect labor cost, overhead and profit margin, all determining the product selling price.) Indirect labor, overhead and margins were applied, and determined in conjunction with the accounting department. This was a bit of learning gained through the paper shuffling at Webcor.

Leonard Koch was our specialist in time study and was very knowledgeable in all operations throughout the plants. He was young, well liked, ambitious and very meticulous. He had reported to the personnel manager before being transferred to Engineering. The two of us seemed to "click" and think alike when it came to time study. At best, it was difficult to achieve uniformity and consistency job after job---study after study. So much depended on attitude, conditions, or feeling of both the operator being timed and the person making the study. As mentioned, this seemingly simple function not only determined profit for the company but it also was directly connected to the earning potential of the worker! With so-called "piece work", if the employee produced more than standard output, they received proportionally increased pay. It was recommended that the company enter into contract with the consulting firm. It proved to be very successful! It was all based on exact tabulation of time required for the "average, normal, healthy human" to make predetermined motions under controlled conditions; such as weight-temperature-atmosphere, etc. Leonard was just outstanding in understanding, implementing, and selling the program to both management and employees! It also improved time and reliability of bidding contract work! Standard costs become much more accurate, variance to standard reduced.

On a lighter side, John Torrison, who was also president of the local country club, asked for my input regarding structures that were being planned for the club. I played a rather minor role, but it enabled me to learn a bit more about the president as an individual not just the boss. I'm sure he was also feeling me out! Through necessity, there was much contact with the treasurer (Mr. Ed Lueck), controller (Mr. Hank Kohlmeyer), plus other officers and managers. This new young engineer was being examined quite closely for a few weeks.

The young Thomsen family of three fell in love with the people and city of Manitowoc. Everyone seemed so friendly and our experience at First Lutheran Church was so rewarding. We made good friends in short order -- Eli with her ever-present smile just acted as a magnet, attracting many as she "presented" our happy daughter, Louise! We were so thankful; this was a "dream and prayer" answered!

CHAPTER 14

Michigan here we come!

1952

Something unexpected came our way in 1952! The Korean War was causing an aluminum shortage. Without normal supply of this "lightweight metal", we had less to sell and remain in business. It was required to seek different products and types of work to supplement aluminum cookware. The company employed Dale Larish, an individual familiar with Washington D.C. and capable and willing to enter into negotiations for military items. Larish, a person from whom I kept my distance did know his way around. We were successful in bidding for the manufacture of 105mm hot forged projectiles for the Army. It did require several trips to Washington, not my favorite place! On one of those trips, to my surprise I came across Mr. Les Kuplic (James Lester Kuplic) with whom I had worked at Kohler Company, then as an industrial engineer. (In 1962, Kuplic became President of Kohler!) He too had obtained a similar contract for the manufacture of a different configuration of the 105mm shell. We traveled together after that to several plants in the U.S. where steel forged projectiles were made for the Army. We later learned that more 105mm shells were fired during the Korean War than in all of World War 2.

With contract in hand, the next step was to lay out the production line, and select all equipment to meet quantity and quality specifications with a specified delivery time in mind. All equipment had to meet with government approval because the "buy American" act was in place at the time. The total equipment price tag amounted to roughly three million in 1952 dollars. This constituted a great challenge! Eli was very supportive, though I was gone many days and nights. Again, what an opportunity for a young engineer with only a few years' experience! Quotations from several suppliers had to be obtained for each item. Ed Irons, purchasing manager at Specialty, was a big help weeding out and obtaining qualified and experienced representatives. Contacts were made and visits scheduled. Shortly after the government approved our contract and we were negotiating purchase of land in Manitowoc for the building required, we received a directive from them that the location of operation would be in Iron Mountain, Michigan. Ford Motor Company had recently shut down and discontinued production of all station wagon models---at that time being made of wooden top side bodies. This plant had been in operation for years there in Iron Mountain; now the city was in dire need of help. My "boss", Vern Hansen and I had to make many trips to the Upper Peninsula (some 75 miles north) to examine, make contacts with local government, and locate contractors and workers. Ford had closed the plant one noontime, just weeks prior, and the plant had been cleared out posthaste. ! Half eaten sandwiches were on the desks, with partially typed letters still in typewriters! Apparently no advanced notice had been given; all were told to leave with their belongings and the gates would be locked soon after 2:00 p.m. Now a massive clean-up was required.

It was my responsibility to lay out the total production line, and establish the flow of product from start to finish. I also had to design the conveying procedures and equipment foundations---everything required to produce the 105 mm projectile per government specifications. I loved it! It was a real challenge and I was thrilled to be a part of it. Eli again was so supportive, allowing me to travel and spend countless hours with outside engineers and suppliers. Often I brought these individuals to our home for dinner.

MICHIGAN HERE WE COME!

On top of all this came another surprise! While working at my drafting board one afternoon, an extreme pain hit me in the right upper chest making breathing almost impossible. An engineer next to me sensed I was having trouble talking and immediately transported me to his doctor! At the hospital it was discovered that one of my lungs had collapsed and immediate attention was mandatory. In just a few days I was back home but was told rest was required and only minimal activity was allowed. This would never do! There was too much to be done at work; for several weeks, work was brought to the house, even suppliers and salesmen came. The body is a wonderful creation! At my still- young age, healing was rapid; the only restriction for about two months was no lifting or strenuous activity, no driving and absolutely no flying. They said I had a "congenital bleb" (A weak spot on the lung that was present at birth and had burst like a small balloon, letting air into my chest cavity). All worked out well and life returned to normal.

Did I say normal? Well, not exactly! Eli delivered our next child, Nancy Kay, on May 3, 1952. Now we both had our hands full. Ha, youth! Looking back on it now makes me tired just to think of it. But, in reality we were having fun, enjoying the wonderful wonders of life and thanking our Lord for so many blessings! Could all of this really be coming to us? Two wonderful and healthy children, an ideal place to live, a workplace with great opportunities and health that permitted us to keep pace. Help abounded at home: Eli's friend Annie Konz, church women, Mom T., neighbors and spring came upon us to brighten most days. God was certainly watching over us, answering many prayers with forgiveness abounding!

In September, 1952, the time had come for Vern Hansen and me to be in Iron Mountain; the plant was clean and ready for modification. Vern was to be the plant manager, and I was to be the plant engineer responsible for installation and tooling, equipment and supervision of quality control. I was also responsible for office, tool room, storage, equipment foundations, utilities-- on and on -- contractors were ready to begin. I also had to find a place for the family to live.

IS GOD ON OUR SIDE?

Just three blocks from the plant entrance, a home was for sale in what was called the "Ford addition". They (Ford Motor Company) had constructed an entire village when setting up production years earlier. Beautifully landscaped and very efficient, this subdivision was in Kingsford, Michigan, but was really a part of Iron Mountain. The price for the home of choice was just under $6,000. The First National Bank of Manitowoc issued the loan being secured by Specialty. The family soon followed me. Annie Konz was there in days; bucket and mop, paint brush in hand. The house would soon become "home" with her help, and the children, well loved, with two great "mothers" at hand.

Kingsford, MI; We Bought It!; Tom is Born!

The old Ford building was converted, with all its conveyors still filled with wood product and obsolete equipment on heavy foundations, removed. Windows gleamed and the new floor was swept meticulously. Gradually, the "new" era was taking over. By rail and truck, shipments began filling the voids; the place was taking shape, employees were smiling. They sure worked hard! At Thanksgiving time, John Torrison paid us a visit. With him were boxes of turkeys, one for each of approximately 20 employees, and a $20 check for each. Never had I witnessed that many grown men with tears in their eyes! In the past, all they had ever experienced at this time of year was a shut down for model change. (Here was another important lesson for a young engineer to place in his memory for the future! A company is as secure and strong as its workers!).

1953

The building we acquired was roughly the size of two football fields---three bays wide, the center bay over 50feet up. An office section on second floor, center-west end, was removed, and our offices were constructed on the first floor far east end . Outside and running the length of the south wall was the rail siding. The two large forging furnaces plus heat treating were fired with Propane gas. Two large gas storage tanks were put in place alongside the rail line. Eight 1000-ton hydraulic presses for hot forging fed the conveyor extending the length of the building and back. There were over twenty automatic, indexers, with carbide tipped tools, hydraulic operated turning lathes. Inside and outside were automatic "shell" painting booths and drying ovens. Everything was set up for as little as possible physical handling of the product; conveyors were everywhere. Employees were predominately Italian and Finish, wonderful and conscientious workers. Our resident government inspector, who had a son fighting in Korea, made sure we produced a perfect "shell".

Iron Nountain 105mm Production Plant

105mm Forged and Machined Artillery Shell

One experience I will never forget! A contractor had finished digging a large pit in a center bay; it was to hold a 10ft X 20ft, 10ft deep "oil quenching tank." The steel tank's arrival was delayed. That evening as I was getting ready for bed at home, a tremendous thunder storm was raging and shaking the house. I quickly drove to the plant to see if all the windows were closed in the office. Walking through the plant I was horrified when going past the "open pit"! The so called soil was "sugar sand"; the storm vibrations were slowly causing the side walls of the pit to collapse, removing the support from under one of the building columns! I had enough exposure to architectural engineers to know that this could cause complete failure of the building structure. The contractor was there in minutes with help and equipment. Thank goodness! Remember, there were no cellphones in those years. The run to the office phone, as I watched the sand gradually sift from under the footing, seemed like hours. The next day we measured the top level of the footing; it had dropped four inches--- a very close call!

Production started ahead of schedule. Our pilot production was taken to the Arsenal for arming of the shells with powder and fuses. All were fired successfully and we were given the OK to start full production! It was a gratifying experience!

An even more rewarding event was to take place for the Thomsen family! On June 20th, 1953, our son, Thomas Wayne Thomsen, was born in Iron Mountain, Michigan! Again Eli's dear friend, Annie Konz, was there to help, putting me to work as only she knew how to do. After all, I think Annie already had three children, on her way to an eventual nine wonderful little ones. Just a superb Christian person and always there when we needed help with the young ones.

Iron Mountain was good to us! We had such wonderful friends, most through the church we joined located in Niagara, not too far south of town. It was a Swedish Covenant Church; so very friendly and "preached" the gospel pure and simple! At first it seemed a bit strange to us; half of the parishioners were very strict, believing in

IS GOD ON OUR SIDE?

Our Family of Five!

no make-up for the gals, and the limited use of some substances. Then the other groups were somewhat "liberal" in their life style. Yet the two groups co-existed in perfect harmony! Two houses west of ours lived the Walter Bietila. He was known here and the world over in the sport of ski-jumping; having won Olympic Gold several times. Wonderful friends!

The community deserves a few lines in the story of my life; it was a delight to experience their friendliness. When I first arrived in town and was living alone, invitations were frequent to join families for meals or activities. I learned in a hurry to not accept every invitation to "come sample my wine!" The Italian people sure knew the art of wine making! It seemed a regular ritual each year for families to combine in the purchase of the grapes. They made a trip to Chicago, selected a train car load of grapes and, after testing for the best grapes, they sent them direct to Iron Mountain. I questioned how they made their selection? They pressed the grape between the palms of their hands, pulled the palms apart and the further you could separate your hands the more sugar the grape contained! A

MICHIGAN HERE WE COME!

very simple procedure. Ask a simple question - get a simple answer! To visit and sample the families' wine entailed a large glass of each batch! And how many were there? Well, I lost count after the third! All kidding aside, it was excellent but I'm not adept at much volume! (I did have to drive home.)

To live in this city it was a must to learn the art of skiing! Children were taught this before walking! Ski jumping? Need you ask? Many jumps could be found in town---jumps off a few feet then a few yards, then watch out, you'd be invited to try Pine Mountain jump. I climbed to the top once. Never again! Wow, you could get hurt up there! Whenever I said that, residents only laughed. Winter sports abounded. Eli and I tried them all; we had fun but the only one we could master was sliding down the hills on a large, old Coke sign used as a sled! This was in the early 1950s, long before "snow coasters" were ever thought of or introduced on the market!

Then there was snow! Not just plain old snow but I mean SNOW! Would it ever stop? Please stop! But to native people it was just plain old beautiful snow! Our house had a garage that was entered from an alley. It was narrow but ample, and always clean. The entire city always seemed clean as a whistle! In the winter snow, I was always able to drive my car out and be to work by 7:00 a.m.! (Try that in Chicago!) People never shoveled the sidewalk in Kingsford, you walked the street! Here I must add, the drivers were much more courteous, slower, knew how to drive in winter. You knew everyone, anyhow, and you're always kind to your friends!

Spaghetti! You had better like it 'cause no matter where you went or ordered you got spaghetti. It was as common as bread and butter! Yes, and it was very good! "Pasties" was another specialty! If you go there, be sure to try it all! And after a full day and a meal, be sure to try a sauna! Especially in the winter with deep snow to jump into after you're boiled and well done (At least pink). This was a great city, with great traditions, and great people that will touch your heart, and make you feel at home. The surrounding area presented exquisite beauty, winter or summer. The ski-jump and slopes would delight you, even if only an "observer.

In the spring of 1953 Specialty brought on board, in Manitowoc, a management consultant to evaluate the business and personnel. After seeing the value of consultants in the "time study" improvement in Manitowoc that worked so well for me, the entrance of Mr. Wes Day from Racine, Wisconsin was welcomed in Iron Mountain. Wes Day impressed me and we became good friends. He was appointed Works Manager for the total company as a consultant. In the spring of 1954, Mr. Day asked if I felt the operation in Iron Mountain was running well enough that I could leave and join him in Manitowoc. I was to be his assistant as well as head of the Engineering Department. Again, opportunity was knocking at our door!

1954

Good memories had been generated in Iron Mountain; what a growing experience for me. I had worked closely with suppliers of machines, tools, and chemicals. I had directed construction and installation with outside contractors. I had met quality specifications in mass production. I had dealt with various local government officials. Most important, I had been a Christian witness. Eli was my ever supportive partner, and what a joy to rear our three healthy children. We had so much to be thankful for! We had made many trips to visit parents on holidays; the back of the car became a bed, and we often left Michigan as the sun was setting. We drove all night as they slept; arriving at grandmother's with the kids still sound asleep! Ah youth! The saying in Iron Mountain was, "This is God's Country". Yes, it was and is.

CHAPTER 15

From Hot Steel Forging Back to Aluminum

1954

April, 1954, saw the Thomsen family once again looking for a place to call home. We found a house at 923 N. 12th St. in Manitowoc, Wisconsin, owned by a family just finishing the construction of a new home and looking for someone to make the house on N. 12th street a home again. A deal was struck, loan and mortgage acquired, and we settled into our new surroundings. Government contracts had become history in my life experience! Or had they! In my absence, another capable engineer, Bob Eierman, with the aid of Jack Harrington (a top notch tool and die person) had set up production of 25mm machine gun links for the U.S. Government. This contract also proved to be successful. It was only a short time and Specialty was back to normal operations, making toys and cookware; aluminum was back on the buyers' markets!

It was great to be back in Manitowoc. The First Lutheran Church was now in a large, beautiful new sanctuary on north 8th Street. When we left for Michigan, this was all in the planning stage. It didn't take long and mother was teaching Sunday school again and I was a deacon. Sunday was known as "Dad's Day" in our house but I think it would have been more accurate to say Sunday morning was "Church Day" with afternoons as "Dad's Day". At any rate we made sure the church was always a good part of our family life.

IS GOD ON OUR SIDE?

Manitowoc Home for 43 years!

Before his ordination, Rev. Roland Schwandt was active in industry, and he was a perfectionist. Before accepting the position of deacon on the church council, it was made very clear what was expected of me: "full support and dedication to the furtherance of the Church!" When he said Church, he meant not just First Lutheran in Manitowoc but the total Christian Church of Christ! This impressed me greatly! It was an honor to serve with some very intelligent and influential people that Pastor had selected for the Church Council. To sit monthly with company officers, owners, and higher education administrators was awesome to a young newcomer in town!

The Council often met at the mansion of Mr. H. L. Vits, seated around a large heavy oak dining table that reminded me of King Arthur's Court. Mr. Vits was Vice President of Mirro Aluminum Company the largest company in town and rival to small Specialty, where I worked. The first meeting for me to attend was held at this beautiful home. It was winter time and the usual snow covering required proper foot ware. I was met at the door by Mr. Vits, a short, stout and stately man. He was very gracious, placing my coat and hat in the spacious coat room. Then he said, "Young man, where are you from, where do you work and what may I ask is your position?" "I'm Dick Thomsen, originally from Chicago, an engineer at Specialty." Quickly he grabbed my hat and coat, shoved them at me, picked up my boots and watched me pull them on, opened the massive front door, pointed and said, "I don't allow company enemies in this house!" I was half way down the long entrance walkway when I heard the loud, deep voice laughing and calling me to "Get back in here, young fellow, if Pastor says you're OK to be in our church, you must be OK for my castle!" From that day on, we were the best of friends. He and his wonderful wife traveled to Phoenix, Arizona, every winter, where my parents were now living. They became good friends after our rather unusual introduction in Manitowoc. Mr. Vits would often call me at work, and invite me to visit the new "Aluminum Rolling Mill" being constructed on the edge of town. It seemed strange that of all people, was with the V.P. of Mirro, getting a tour of this competitor's 8 million dollar facility under construction.

At the office, work was always a challenge; the plant at Chilton was having space problems---that is, lack of space. We had bid on contract work that required some new equipment which could also supplement present product production. To accommodate this, a building expansion was completed. My construction knowledge was growing.

Two men at Specialty influenced my life and became very close friends. Henry Kohlmeyer, the controller who later became Treasurer, was so helpful in fulfilling the government contracts. My limited knowledge of book keeping and finance acquired at college was a big help, enabling me to at least sound intelligent. Henry appreciated it and went out of his way to help me gain more. He became a second father to my son, Tom. His personality was a natural for family life. Whenever he was in our home the children were attracted to him as a magnet. He never married---had only a sister living in Sheboygan and two nieces living some distance away. Tomas Gannon, sales manager of toys and decorations, had come to the company from Montgomery Ward, Chicago. He and Hank worked closely together in surprising improvements in the toy division. Somehow I was accepted into their confidence, and we became known as the working trio!

Early on, John Torrison had convinced me to join the Branch River Country Club. Reluctant for some time, it was soon evident he expected it, so I joined. (Interesting, my paycheck showed an increase the very next week.) The threesome was found at the BRCC every stag afternoon plus Saturday mornings for a round or two of golf. While this was an activity that kept us healthy, there were three subjects that brought us very close together: Family, work, and religion. The Gannon and Thomsen families were much alike, our children were loving and close; Henry was very well liked and just loved children. All three men had families that were strong in their beliefs; two Protestant and, one, Catholic (Gannons). We often discussed our faith; we could easily agree that all were strong Christians and respected the others' position. The bond between the three of us became very strong for the rest of our lives. At one time consideration was given for the three starting our own consulting firm, that of advising officials of troubled companies on how to improve their operations.

It was soon evident that the cookware industry, as well as the toy industry, was extremely competitive! Profit margins trended to the slim side. New innovations were a key to improved profits but to develop that "something new" was a real challenge! Working with the sales people was always a challenge in itself. They tended to be extroverts and outgoing types; engineers tended toward the opposite. They were slow to move until facts were spelled out in order: 1-2-3. This constituted another learning curve for me. It took time, but, in due time, appreciation soaked in. Another way to increase that profit margin was to be more efficient in how we made that mundane pot or pan. I felt this cost reduction was in large part my responsibility and where I should focus my time. With the help of people like Lenard Koch and Wes Martin, it proved to be fun, not just work! There was a staff of five in the engineering department at that time. We were kept very busy; when "sales" came up with a new product, drawings had to be made from which tools and dies were designed. Then came first production runs, packaging design, sample models, specifications of purchased components, and estimated labor hours to produce the items. Add to this the new task of reducing the existing labor and material cost of any or all products now being sold!

One example of how improvements were made in both labor and material costs.

Muffin Pan." (6 cup unit)

OLD PRODUCTION METHOD

A. (6 cups) (Six small individual pans required, each requiring 4 operations)

1. blank-draw (stamping press, 1 operator)
2. Spin-trim (speed lathe, 1 operator)
3. Wash (water washing machine, 1 operator)
4. Crate & store (1 trucker)

B. (1 Frame to hold the 6 cups) (requires 3 operations to make)

1. Blank-draw-imprint (stamping press, 1 operator)
2. Wash (water washing machine, 1 operator)
3. Crate & store (1 trucker)

C. (6 cups assembled to 1 frame) requires 2 operations

1. Bring cups & frames to press room (1 trucker)
2. Place 6 cups in 1 frame press together. (Power press, 1 operator)

For many years it took a total of 6 operations (6 operators) and 3 trucking people to get this product ready to package.

NEW PRODUCTION METHOD

A. Total unit made all in one piece. (Requiring 3 operations)

1. Blank-flange-imprint. (Stamping press, 1 operator)

2. Spin cups in blanked unit (special spin machine, 1 operator)

3. Wash (water washing machine, 1 operator)

Comparison of OLD to NEW!

	OLD METHOD	**NEW METHOD**
Operations	6	3
Operators	6	3
Trucking	3	0

To accomplish this savings, there was a cost up front. I scheduled a trip to Canada to witness a similar operation being performed by a firm that manufactured completely different products. I had to take pictures of the operation and then described it to a machine designer. Then we contracted to have the machine built, tested and purchased.

FROM HOT STEEL FORGING BACK TO ALUMINUM

We took the design and had the machine shop build the tooling to stamp-flange-imprint the aluminum sheet. The cost of the change was paid for in less than two years. This constituted a good return on investment that soon increased profit on the thousands of products produced for years in the future. (It also improved the appearance and function of the product.)

Not all projects could show this type and degree of improvement. Yes, we laid a few eggs here and there, but you learn that the degree of success is in direct proportion to risks taken. As an engineering team, we enjoyed our work. We even let the women in our lives give us a hand! The Kochs, Martins and Thomsens had many get-togethers at our homes. A little coffee and sweets did help, but much time was spent brainstorming what could be done to improve cooking in the kitchen. One item idea we came up with was the "juice saver" lip on pie pans! Someone said, "Last night when I baked the cherry pie, it bubbled over onto the oven bottom! How could that be corrected? The idea of the extra lip on pie pans was the result! Yes, we did come up with some winners and we had fun doing it!

CHAPTER 16

Artificial Christmas Trees? Of Aluminum?

1959

The ideas for new products were frequently generated by sales-marketing individuals or by the customer. One that became very successful was presented to us engineers by Tom Gannon in late 1958 early '59. Could we make an artificial Christmas tree that could sell for $20.00 or less? Of course it had to be made of aluminum! Tom had seen a handmade tree while in the Chicago area, presented the concept to us and wheels were set in motion. By Christmas of 1959 we were in production and shipping trees throughout the country. In 1960, demand increased, requiring added factory space. Teamwork spread to include metal suppliers, machine design and construction, protective and economical packaging, training of employees, advertising strategy, complimentary items such as lighting, music and rotating tree stands; the list grew, sales grew and profit followed. The aluminum Christmas tree was a big winner for the company, thanks to the foresight of Mr. Gannon, his marketing know-how, and knowledge of the decoration industry. Not only did he inspire buyers but also the team at home to purchase the product designed to be attractive to the public. Gannon was a wonderful leader who kept us all excited to see success in motion.

Aluminum Specialty Company was growing; and it moved from being a family owned entity to public ownership through issuing

Aluminum Christmas Trees?

stock and being traded on the open market. Ed Luick, Vice President of Finance, invited me to become a member of a small investment group that studied and invested in the stock market. With each person adding monthly dollars to the pool, round lots of stock could be purchased on a regular basis, reducing the broker fees to a minimum. (Online wireless technology was never even a dream at that time!) Each member would select and report on stocks they felt had potential. This required research, the creation of graphs, and a short presentation to the group. My Dad often spoke of his expertise in market transaction. This was a new welcome source of learning in addition to conversation with my consultant father: "Mr. Experience". It was also the beginning of the "Dick-Eli" thinking and planning for the future. Father was a tremendous influence when it came to investing and very knowledgeable in regard to the stock market and insurance.

1. "Start as soon as you can to put aside a percentage of your income on a regular basis and let it grow!"

2. When investing, "Diversify, don't put all your eggs in one basket!"

As I look back on these times, I realize how fortunate I was to have been with such a fine management group where I could freely express myself, be among Christian fellow workers and share in both winning and losing conditions without trepidation. A young engineer was learning at a steady pace from qualified family and friends.

1960

The action at the home front was not much different! Now we were a family of five. Louise was going on ten, with Nancy and Tom, just a few steps behind. Mother was the real worker here! She was up each morning very early to see that Tippy was attended to. Tippy was the cocker spaniel given to the children when just a cute little puppy. We couldn't refuse accepting the little handful from a neighbor girl on a Sunday as we returned from church. Other exciting times: Louise, with one of four kidneys having to be removed in surgery; Nancy, looking like a little clown with most of her hair falling out; Tom, with a seizure which brought Dr. Bob running to the house where he plopped little Tom into a snow bank to reduce the high fever! Add to all of this her endless list of church responsibilities plus giving of her love which seemed endless.

The short list doesn't do Eli justice. She was Sunday school teacher for the cradle roll for at least 25 years. She sent letters to each child up until high school age to remind them of their baptism, which she labeled "Christian Birthday." She joined the Snip & Sew club, which she ended up leading for years. She was a summer bible school leader, LDR member, Bethel Bible grad, new member co-chair with me, kitchen co-chair, coffee service assistant, Men's brotherhood meal maker, women's guild worker, lap robe maker and distributor, co-organizer of "missionary for a day," co-leader and leader of the Children's Christmas program ----- I know there are more but you get the idea.... Oh, I can't forget one of the most cherished roles: hospital and home visitor for shut-ins, and she even took the role "Power of Attorney" for some prominent old time members. Eli was a smiling giver of self! I really think the five of us spent as much time at church or church work as we did at home. Luther League, camps, outings, choirs, scouts, Sunday school--- I suppose it was of necessity for the children, with mother and dad so active in church doings. I served as president, vice president, and chairman of Deacons, finance, and call committees. I also taught in Sunday school and Bethel, I was district representative, served as pastoral counseling and support; I was on constitution update committees and served as laymen Sunday coordinator. I participated in building painting and cleanups, senior choir, hospital visitation, and visitation to every new Manitowoc resident. It was the services I really enjoyed, mostly as a result of encouragement from Eli in our daily prayer together.

ARTIFICIAL CHRISTMAS TREES? OF ALUMINUM?

What a wonderful support she was in all that I attempted or anticipated, planned or rejected, studied or reviewed. There is no mistaking it---our Christian relationship was our great secret in a wonderful life together and with others. While on the subject of Eli and her expertise: she inherited from her mother a love for cooking, baking, canning. She was very happy when I brought home all verities of aluminum cook- and bake ware! And the four of us received the benefits!) When day was done for the young ones, you would often find mother sitting at the foot of the wrought iron railing stairway where the business desk was conveniently located. There she listened for "what was not to be taking place" upstairs! While there, she kept records of all purchases and everything of importance that had taken place that day (all in the little Blue Book). In the early days, Eli was private secretary to the president of a bond firm in the downtown Chicago Loop (in the Field building just across from the Banker's building, where brother, Jack, and I worked). She knew well how to keep records and how investments were made, recorded, and kept track of. On payday, the check was handed to Eli. She made the deposits, and kept the records. Anything over and above what was needed till the next check, was invested in the Money Market, then to CD's when the quantity was sufficient. She kept track of every bank in town and what interest rate was highest! I not only had a "wife and mother" but the best of "private secretaries!"

Our social life hinged around my Christian business friends as mentioned before and Eli's friends dating, for most part, to her LDR times. These young ladies brought us husbands together as well. Many evening gatherings in various homes saw us all singing hymns around the piano or organ. Of course coffee and homemade goodies were always in abundance! Fry outs were common. Again, most was related to our church affiliation. One very close family from church was the Bohrers! Louise and Egon, along with daughter, Linda, and son, Tim, just fit "our style" in every respect! He and I were both active in the church and with our pastors. Eli and Louise were both very active in church activities. Even the kids hit it off well. We enjoyed many weekend trips to parks or their lake cottage; even on below-zero days, we bundled up to look like Eskimos. Off we would go to walk the frozen river. During the summer time, it was always Louise Bohrer's famous chicken for lunch in the park or tailgating parties on their station wagon..

5/10/1962

Just cried the night after my birthday-- so many dear friends --all so anxious to show their interest and were so thoughtful in sharing my day on Monday. Cards, gifts, visit -- it was a most wonderful day. Jewels to tuck in the crown of memory.

8/9/1962

-- Dick hears so much of unhappy marriages in the office and those who want to separate - you begin to wonder if you are foreign being so very happy together. There's where a good faith shared and lived makes the difference!

12/14/1962

--- Christmas Eve services and Christmas Day service - we will spend The Christ Child's birthday in the House of the Lord - and then quietly enjoy each other as a family. We will share together the joys of dear loved ones that are ours, good health, good home, good job, happiness and many friends and necessities more than we need. Just the wonderful joy of a Christian family at home together!

The church had their annual Advent concert last Sunday -- so proud of our girls as they sang -- no better way to start the Advent season -- preparing for Christmas -- what grand memories to cherish!

Dec 18, 1962

Sunday, a most sacred and lovely concert at church. Thrilled to share Christ in music. Our hearts were filled with the joyous loving sounds -- worship together -- this is Christmas – Christ's birthday and we are so happy for these moments shared with the children.

Eli

Lesson #6

When blessings abound be sure to give thanks;
He is waiting for you!

CHAPTER 17

"Small Business Partnership" -- Another New Adventure

1963

Early in 1963, a friend whom I had met at the Country Club and also a new member of our church, asked us to their home for an evening. Conversation led to a discussion of his company. Chet Heiden and family had come to Manitowoc several years earlier and bought out the sheet metal business from the Krescher brothers. It was a fabrication shop, mainly bidding on heating and ventilating contracts for industries and homes. After some preliminaries, it soon became evident why the invitation of the evening. He asked if I would be interested in joining the firm as a partner. He had one other partner, Tom Hauge, who had worked for the Mirro Company. I was soon to find out that Tom was an excellent engineer, experienced in tools and dies as well as machine design. Chet Heiden was looking to expand the business. I was intrigued by the request, did some research, talked with the attorney, and received financial statements of the rather new F. C. Heiden Inc.

To make the move required considerable cash. To be part owner, the price was set based on the book value. Mr. Heiden would retain controlling interest, owning 51% of the total value. Tom had a percent figure and the remaining was available for me to purchase. Ever since working with brother, Jack, the idea of being in business for me was planted in my mind as a future objective. This was a viable challenge to be considered!

On a weekend church sponsored "boy scout" camping trip with son, Tom, a fellow deacon, Bob Berkedahl, was also there with his son. As usual, when we were together, conversation drifted to our livelihood or church calls. I mentioned the possible job change. He knew Chet Heiden, and when the subject of my need for money came up, Bob casually stated that his retired father was looking for a place to invest some cash at a very reasonable interest rate. On February, 1963, a contract with Chet Heiden was signed; notice was given to Aluminum Specialty of my decision. Mr. Berkedahl gave me a loan, money was borrowed on life insurance and stock now owned as a result of "club investments" used as collateral for a bank loan. I was now part owner of a business!

F. C. Heiden Co., Manitowoc, WI.

Eli was a vital part of all this! She was just as excited; we both were thrilled. My business financial experience was at a medium level, so I had consulted with friend, Hank Kohlmeyer, for hours at our home, and Eli was present for much of this. Another person who was also much involved was our dear Pastor at First Lutheran, but at a very different level. Eli knew from our first mention of marriage,

"SMALL BUSINESS PARTNERSHIP" -- ANOTHER NEW ADVENTURE

and from my early thoughts before time served in the Army, that being a minister was "high on my list" of service. Inquiry and application had been made at the Luther Seminary in St. Paul, Minnesota. Pastor Anderson had helped us in this decision. Two new "adventures" had been placed in front of the Thomsen Family. An answer was not forthcoming; we prayed and waited. The answer came in a strange way. Pastor called me in regard to some church visitation or concerns; we met and, before parting, he asked of our decision.

"We are still not sure," I said.

His reply made the difference. "Dick, you know you can be a worker for Christ as a businessman just as influentially as standing in a pulpit! Plus, you have three young children to think of in their formative years."

2/14/63

-- Dick and I feel as if the heavens were opened and God forgot to halt the flow of blessings to us. We feel overwhelmed with the good fortune and joy that is ours -- Oh, if we could just share it there with you -- what a thrill. We feel burdened with the joy of blessings that are ours - we can't deserve even a small part of it - talking with Pastor and praying much. On Feb. 2nd - Dick, I and partner, God, signed the official papers -- the Lord was overly generous to bless us with such a tremendous opportunity.

It was only one day after starting work at Heiden's that the Kohler Company called at the house, leaving a message for me to call a Mr. James Leslie Kuplic. He was an industrial engineer I had worked with, the same person with whom I traveled to learn the process of making 105mm shells for the Army, the person who had become

IS GOD ON OUR SIDE?

President of the Kohler Company in 1962. He wanted to interview me for the position of V.P. Engineering. Thank goodness this did not come earlier! Little doubt, I would have wanted the position if offered. Just five years later, 1968, Les Kuplic died of a heart attack. The new president replaced the position (along with many others) with his own choices. Was it luck? I doubt it. Then I was honored and thankful those years later, to see that the hand of someone greater than me had been working in the background.

It was during this very hectic year that Eli's parents were experiencing health problems. Living in their comfortable home was becoming difficult; mother Zapel was having mental lapses and George, her father, was not that physically capable of handling mother in addition to what was required around the house. Eli's brother, Russ, called us one day and, together, it was arranged for Dad and Mom to live with us in Manitowoc. We had the room and what a wonderful chance for the children to be with their grandparents! It really worked well, although now I realize it had to be a tremendous work load on Eli. She took it all in stride and never missed a beat in looking after the house, attending church activities, and doing all the finance bookwork as usual! With three bedrooms and one bath, it was a little strain on space and timing.

Cash was short but cash flow was still OK. We had no problem paying monthly bills and for that we were so thankful. In talking with Russ, it was agreed that we could add to our house with the financial help of the senior Zapels. We added a bedroom upstairs and family room below. Construction began in July, 1963, and it provided interest for Grandpa George, lots of excitement for the kids, dust for mom, and a few concerns for dad (yours truly) who always seemed to want changes from what the architect had specified. Working now for the Heiden Company was of some help, as we were in the sheet metal-heating-roofing contractor business. All was completed rather rapidly and successfully. Before carpet was laid in the family room, I recall several "young people" roller skating on the plywood floor! Yes with mom and dad's permission.

"SMALL BUSINESS PARTNERSHIP" -- ANOTHER NEW ADVENTURE

The 2 ½ years spent at "Heidens" went very quickly. The company grew quite consistently, Tom Haug was a terrific engineer, and it was a real pleasure working and learning with him. Since I was known at Kohler, good contracts for work resulted. Designing special machines was the most interesting aspect of the job. Operations, managing, and planning in a small business was much different from my past employment opportunities. Over half of my time was spent in rather repetitive work. For example, a farmer needed a new fender for his old Deere tractor. How much would it cost and how soon? Not sure this was a real challenge.

One good thing that was happening: There was more time for the family. The children were growing up so fast! Louise was a teenager. My experience at Kohler also paid off; heating and ventilating price quotes utilized the knowledge gained in the design group for the cast iron finishing plant. We did extensive work for Rahr Malting and Mirro Corporation here in Manitowoc. I thought it a bit strange that, on several occasions, officers from Mirro would pay a visit to Chet Heiden, asking for a tour of our one-floor shop. As mentioned, Mr. Vits and I had become good friends via church council meetings. I was familiar with the other officers through casual meetings at the country club. My parents had become good friends of Mr. and Mrs. H. L. Vits of Mirro. They spent their winters in Phoenix, Arizona and visited my parents frequently.

CHAPTER 18

Not Always "What You Know" but "Who You Know" That Counts!

1965

In May of 1965, I had a surprise visit from Mr. Wes Day, the consultant with whom I had worked at Iron Mountain and at Aluminum Specialty, Manitowoc. At lunch he asked if I would consider moving to a new job. It would mean moving family again but he assured me it would be well worth it! The idea of uprooting the family again was unattractive, to say the least. We had great friends, a fine church, a very happy family and a beautiful home of our dreams. Wes proceeded with a few details. He said it was a large, well known company. My engineering experience plus associated business background would fit well. Potential for advancement was there. He suggested we get together again soon, after I had a chance to talk with Eli. He knew how close we were as a couple and that she would have equal say in any such dramatic move.

I gave Eli the news that evening after the family was in bed. We were both a bit stunned and full of questions for each other. Was it even right or good to ask the kids to give up their friends, and start over at a strange school. How would it affect their health and their preparation for the future? These were matters we did not have to face before as a family---the children were much younger then! We

IS GOD ON OUR SIDE?

had just gone through this bit. Why now? Our wish to be owners of a small business was now a reality; should we give all that up? Yet we knew our future hinged on the decision made. Yes, we asked for guidance in prayer; that had become a normal place to rest our hope and trust. We also knew answers came in unexpected ways and at unlikely times. At our next soon meeting, I hesitated a bit, but finally told Mr. Day,, " No, we just think it too soon for our family to pick up stakes. It would be too disruptive for the children and not fair to them."

Mr. Day half-smiled at our answer and quickly commented. "I rather expected that answer from you two! Before accepting that as your final word, let me explain a bit more about the potential new position. You would be general manager of a rather large engineering department; and you would report to the VP of operations. This VP is approaching retirement; if you perform as expected, you could be in the running to step up." With that information, Mr. Day advised that we meet again soon: "I do not want you to give me a definite answer of yes or no, just tell me if you are willing to consider moving and we can talk more about what is entailed."

Two days later our reply was delivered: "Yes, if all is as you indicate, we are interested and would consider the move with the family." I had worked with this gentleman enough in the past to know and recognize his smiles and expressions, plus I respected his judgment and sincerity.

He answered, "I had to know for sure if you and Eli were really interested enough in moving ahead to even move from Manitowoc with your family and away from your church and all the good things you have here. Now that I see you're truly that willing to advance, it's time for you to know the rest of the story. The president of this company would like to interview you tomorrow morning at 10:00 am in his office on the 7th floor, Mirro Aluminum Company. Mr. A. L. Vits, President-Chairman Of the Board and CEO is expecting you. Don't be late."

NOT ALWAYS "WHAT YOU KNOW" BUT "WHO YOU KNOW" THAT COUNTS! ➤

"BIG" Mirro Aluminum Co.

We couldn't believe it! I think Eli was just as surprised as I. We could stay in our wonderful home and all that came with it; what an opportunity! God had answered and blessed us once more. My concern now was: can I sell myself to Mr. A. Vits? Mirro was the largest employer in the area. Never did I dream that I might work for this great company---the leader in the cookware industry, a trade name known throughout the world. It was difficult to get any sleep that night! A letter written by Eli a few days later captures our feelings better than any words I could possible write today!

June 28, 1965

Dear family,

Our lives have once again been richly blessed through prayer. At times, hard to always accept the will of God -- and thus I think the saying, "Prayer changes us", is better than "Prayer changes things." We must be changed to fit the calling of the Spirit. For, once we yield to His calling, we find the strength, ability, zeal, knowledge that we need for the

IS GOD ON OUR SIDE?

> *task of living. Prayer has led us in so many ways -- couldn't relate them all -- but has been a very real experience for us all along in our married life.*
>
> *In these last months, it has been prayer most earnestly that has led Dick in big decisions for the future -- and we feel we have had the answer -- like a bombshell -- and now move forward into a new future of work opportunities. Only Dick's business partner and our Pastor know that Dick has resigned his job; soon the announcement will be made in the local paper. Yes, Dick has a new job -- one that in our greatest dreams we never hoped for -- almost scares Dick with the responsibility. Dick was sought out for the job -- again, the answer of the Spirit in our prayers. As some know, we were deciding if he should go into the ministry -- and for many months we have been seeking answers to our decision. The Spirit came through like a bombshell. This was not the only job offered, 2 others with great opportunity and challenge, -- almost emotionally wrung dry, but most humble in that we have been so blessed, led by the Spirit and feel such a surge of strength and joy in our new planning.*
>
> *Dick has been hired by Mirro Aluminum Company as director of all engineering. They have 3 plants here in Manitowoc, 2 in Two Rivers and 3 plants including a large Rolling Mill between the two cities. We are breathless. We cry with undeserved joy! Greatly humbled by the opportunity that has been offered.*
>
> *Much Love, Eli*

At 10:00 in the morning I was led and I must admit, a bit nervously, to the corner office of Mr. A. Vits.

NOT ALWAYS "WHAT YOU KNOW" BUT "WHO YOU KNOW" THAT COUNTS!

He soon put me at ease and it was apparent that he had a complete run down on my past employment. This was the person that had hired the consultant, Mr. Wes Day, whom I had worked with at Aluminum Specialty. I had to be nervous, considering the large and auspicious office on the top (7th floor) of the tallest and biggest office building in town. Exposure was on the southeast corner, overlooking the city of Manitowoc. Meeting with the President and Chairman of the Board of the Mirro Aluminum Company was not an everyday occurrence for a young engineer. (I must mention, this Mr. A. L. Vits was the brother of H. L. Vits who was a Vice President of the company and friend from my church.)

Questions centered on why I would consider changing from ownership in a business to that of working for someone else? He asked, "What makes you think you are qualified to manage our large engineering department?" I don't remember what my answers were but do know the conversation appeared to please him. My questions came to the surface too: What type of engineering was involved and who would I be reporting to?

"You will be reporting to the Vice President of manufacturing, Mr. Ralph J. Paddock; You will have the title of Manager of Engineering which covers product design, packaging design and estimating, industrial engineering, tool and die design and procurement, and plant engineering, including buildings, equipment, machinery and maintenance." The present manager was to retire in several weeks.

Having changed jobs a few times, I had learned how to set all the ground rules before shaking hands in acceptance. I had to make sure that all bases were touched before going home! Salary had been confirmed before agreeing to the interview but there had been no mention of vacation time. Finally, I said, "It is very obvious, Mr. Vits, that you know every detail of my past work experience. Yes, you even related how I was able to set up, manage, and get into production a complete new plant for your competitor, including facilitation of design and cost estimation of new products. You were completely aware that in the past few years I became part-owner of my own business. It would appear you are looking for someone with experience to fill a void in your organization. What is your policy for employees with my length of experience regarding vacation time?" With no hesitation, he told me I had a month of vacation per year. (Note of interest: I never recall using up all of my vacation time from my first to the last day at any position, even throughout the 18-plus years with Mirro!)

Near the end of our interview, Mr. Vits asked very bluntly, "What are your ambitions and goals here at Mirro?" I had been warned by the consultant in advance that this question would more than likely be asked. "Sir, I want your job!"

With that, he stood up, shook my hand and said, "You're hired! I have but one word of advice. Don't move too fast, I still am too young to retire. You'll have to work a little while yet." Another request was that nothing was to be said for three weeks. They wanted to make proper arrangements for the retiring manager of engineering, plus planning my announcement. He did agree to my having a confidential meeting with Mr. John Torrison Sr., President of Aluminum Specialty who had become a very good friend and now "a competitor." I also had to negotiate with my partner, Chet Heiden. This proved to be another big lesson in my life experience. "Handshakes are fine but always get important matters in writing, too".

Before leaving Mr. A Vits office, he called in V.P. Ralph Paddock, Senior V.P. Manufacturing, Fred Terens and Senior V.P. Marketing & Sales, Garhart Kubits. I had met them before at Branch River Country Club; they all had big welcoming smiles; it was very obvious they had been waiting in the wings to enter for congratulations and warm handshakes. "We all knew Ally Vits would approve in short order, "Welcome aboard the Mirro Team!"

Chet Heiden was a good friend. We had worked well together and respected each other. He worked hard, played hard and was no

NOT ALWAYS "WHAT YOU KNOW" BUT "WHO YOU KNOW" THAT COUNTS!

pushover when it came to dollars and cents. It was not well received when I told him I'd been offered a position with tremendous future potential and wanted to sell my interest in the company back to him. "What company are you going with? You can't do this!" After settling down, he said we would have to meet with the attorney. A big mistake was made on my part to have used his attorney when the contract was made in the beginning to become a partner in the firm. This time I acquired my own separate attorney who quickly pointed out the original agreement did not contain a buy and sell clause. This meant that I was at Chet's mercy as to what he could pay to buy back my interest.

His first offer was extremely low in comparison to what I had gone in debt for and had paid him. I winced, and he said, "Well Dick, what then do you think is a fair price?" Being a partner, a financial statement was available. I also consulted with my attorney and asked advice of my friend, Henry Kollmeyer from Specialty. A fair price based on book value was in my pre-determined answer book. Again the Good Lord was watching over me; Chet never flinched. He just said, "That's fine by me!" An honest man indeed! In short order my loans were paid off and Eli and I were again debt free except for the house! Later on when Chet found out where I was to work, I'm sure he was very happy he had agreed to my terms; much work from Mirro came to the Heiden Company where I would have control as to who was awarded contracts!

This move was overwhelming, to say the least. It was difficult to remain silent for three weeks, as requested. To help prevent my spilling the beans, Eli suggested I take a trip to visit my parents in Phoenix. June is not the best time for visiting that part of the country, but with air conditioning it would be a great place for me to relax.

On June 16th, 1965 (eight days before my 41st birthday) Mirro Aluminum Company became my new challenge, one that I had never dreamed could happen! Looking back, there seemed to be a pattern in my life that was difficult to explain or grasp. I felt confident in my ability to handle this new position; how fortunate to have had so many good people to guide and teach me; to recommend and speak for me; to open doors that seemed out of reach. And I was blessed to have a dear companion such as Eli, that faithfully supported me and, most of all, prayed with me each night! How could this be happening to me! It seemed that "God was on my side"---at least He was asked to be and requests were made that He guide us; Eli and I could hardly believe all that was happening, but were very thankful!

Lesson #7

It's not always What you Know but Who You Know!
(Especially God!)

CHAPTER 19

That Word, "Aluminum", Now Back in Our Lives!

1965

After the three weeks of silence, that first day of work was something to remember! Vice President, Ralph Paddock, took me to my glass walled office which overlooked the long row of engineering drafting tables. Two large windows were at my back, on the outside east wall. It overlooked the downtown area of the city and a view of Lake Michigan! I was on the top floor, where all the corporate offices were located. The rather spacious office contained several visitors' chairs, a large desk, very comfortable swivel armed chair, a large reference table behind me and several filing cabinets within easy reach. This kind of luxury was all new to me! It was located behind the 6th and 7th window from the north wall and elevator as one would see it from the ground level outside. As one walked further down this long hallway to the south, one passed offices of the Personnel Manager, an outside consultant's office, Vice President Ralph Paddock's office, Senior Vice President Fred Teren's and finally in the corner office, where I had been interviewed, was Mr. Albert L. Vits, President and Chairman of the Board. All of the offices were furnished in good taste and the trim was done in beautifully finished hardwood, augmented with fine arts and rich carpeting. It all reminded me of what you witnessed on the movie screen when portraying the largest and best of industries! I was impressed!

It's difficult for me to express my thankfulness and gratitude for Mr. Paddock. From that first day, he seemed to grease the path for me; to this day I admire his willing attitude in conveying useful information, history of and introduction to tasks that were in front of us. He openly asked me to work with him as a team, to take what he had worked to accomplish and add to it in tandem. He was a graduate engineer, and we seemed to "speak the same language". I had the feeling from the beginning that he was adopting me as a son; again how fortunate I was. But it wasn't all peaches and cream. It was quickly brought to my attention that this company always had promoted from within! To bring in an outsider was unheard of and, of all things, I was a person who had worked for a competitor!

Let me go back to that first day. After quickly showing me my workplace, Mr. Paddock led me past all the empty desks and offices, into a large conference room where it appeared that the entire 7th floor had gathered. I mean everyone was present: Sales -Marketing - Purchasing - Finance - Accounting - Engineers - Personnel - Office Manager - Credit-Secretaries - Security. Everyone had assembled, waiting for President Vits to introduce me and spell out my responsibilities and my credentials. Wow! This was beyond my imagination! When it was over, all came forward to welcome me and shake my hand. It had to be difficult for some of them: this was a company that always promoted from within and, for a past competitor to move in at this level of management was absolutely not the norm. My work was cut out for me; I had to gain their respect.

The rest of the day was spent with Ralph Paddock and a tour of the main plant in Manitowoc. The days following were a continuation of that grand tour, until all plants were visited and I was introduced to plant management. I can hardly express how wonderful and helpful the late Ralph Paddock was to me. Right from the beginning he took me in like I was his son. My new boss was so willing to convey in complete confidence his feelings regarding persons and conditions, how he was planning the future as he saw needs for the company, suggestions for me to follow. All this was very helpful as I began my new adventure.

Touring the many plants of Mirro took more days than I had ever imagined. Ten plants in total added up to over two million square feet of floor space with at least 3,000 employees! Four of these plants were located in Manitowoc, two in Two Rivers (8 miles north), three located between the two cities and one in Oconomowoc, Wisconsin. As we traveled to each of these areas, we got to know each other quite well and I believe this to be reason for our eventual common respect. His Christian faith impressed me! He also loved his work, respected the worker and was, best of all, (just kidding here but true to my training) a graduate engineer! (Chemical Engineer from Ohio State Univ., B.S. plus Masters of Science.) He had a 39-year career with Mirro so he knew every little detail of its history, growth, and people and had strong feelings as to what required attention in the future.

One of those concerns made an impression on me and became an objective of my own for the rest of my years at Mirro. Ralph was what is commonly called a people person. He felt everyone had a right to their own opinion and should be heard. He coupled this with a deep respect for the workers, as well as for the management of the company. The frequent Labor Union strikes disturbed him deeply; he could see that these actions were devastating to both parties and to the future of both. He hoped and asked of me a concerted effort in finding a solution compatible to both sides if and when I were ever to be in a position to do so. Little did I realize that this day would come, and not too far in the future. First, let me return to our visitation of the ten plants.

It was Mr. Paddock's intent to introduce me to the plant management of each of these operating units and where their office was located. In Manitowoc, the main office, then identified as Plant #2, appeared to have been constructed over a period of years in six

IS GOD ON OUR SIDE?

different stages, distinguished by structural materials and covering a full city block. The last unit constructed was seven stories high; the tallest in the city of Manitowoc. Mr. Larry Cooper was the plant superintendent, his office and staff located on the 5th floor. With introductions completed, I was invited to call any time and be given a complete tour. This routine continued from plant to plant; needless to say, my head was swimming after five or six days of this walking and meeting of people. Fortunately, Ralph had given me a copy of the company phone directory making it possible for me to make notes and to study during evenings at home. Everyone was most friendly and appeared happy to welcome an outsider to the Mirro family. Four of the plants were undergoing major expansions at the time; Plant#1 and #4 fabrication, Two Rivers: Plant#6, Rolling Mill; and finally the Boat Plant adjacent to Plant#2 in Manitowoc. Mirro Aluminum Company was proving to be much larger and complex than I had ever imagined. This year sales stood at a new high of $59.2 Million.

After these whirlwind tour days, it was a pleasure to locate a bit more stably in my new office atmosphere! I'm quite sure my staff of six men was more than anxious to hear from me and find out who this outsider really was. We had not met before my being appointed on June 16th . It was possible for me to review their history and for Mr. Paddock to brief me previous to this meeting.

> Estimating -- Louis Berkovits
> Tool & Die Design -- Ernest Greycarek
> Manufacturing Engineering & Research -- Elmer Torke
> Plant Engineering -- George Anderson
> Electronic Engineering -- Anthony Packowski

All had been with Mirro for extended years and had been recognized for their achievements. It was a group packed with tremendous knowledge and experience. The main emphasis in our first meeting together was to assure them that I looked to them for controlling and making decisions in their everyday areas of responsibility and I would back them 100%. I expected them to keep me informed and they should feel free to see me at any time. I would need their help, suggestions, and backing as I learned and attempted to be a person they could trust to be fair in all respects. It was a fine group of five excellent men who worked well together and it was very evident that they were individuals that were well respected by plant personnel.

My experience and training gained in the previous fifteen years served me very well in evaluating the responsibilities of each of the individuals. How they performed those tasks could only be determined over time. From all information I had it was evident that each person was very capable and effective. Evaluation of each responsibility as I saw it follows:

> Estimating: Berkovits and his staff established labor and material cost to produce and package product. They accumulated data from purchasing, accounting, tool & die engineering, methods and time study, packaging and sales. Also they correlated matters with the accounting department on burden rates. Margins were not their responsibility.

> Tool & Die Design: When presented with an approved product design, they would determine operation sequence, equipment to be used and the tooling required to produce the components. It was also their decision regarding where the tooling was to be made, whether through outsourcing or in-house. Consultation with the machine shop was required. Material grade and size were specified. Greycarik was very qualified and respected, with a wealth of experience and knowledge, and he supervised a staff of outstanding tool and die designers.

> There were three tool and die shops, under the control of corresponding plant superintendent at plants #1,2 and 6.

> Manufacturing Engineering & Research: -- Elmer Torke was a graduate chemical engineer from the University of Wisconsin.

IS GOD ON OUR SIDE?

He had been with Mirro for 11 years, and was very instrumental in the development of Teflon application at Mirro. Since Teflon was a very costly material he continually monitored its application and usage. The same applied to all finishes and coatings such as paint, chemicals, anodizing, plating, buffing, lubricants, or any new process. A very capable and reliable engineer, Elmer had all the makings for further advancement in the organization.

Plant Engineering: -- George Anderson was unbelievable in his knowledge of every nook and cranny in every plant. Oversaw new construction, maintenance of all facilities (buildings and machinery) and grounds.

Electronic Engineering: -- Packowski was a specialist! Any electronic device was his responsibility to maintain or recommend. As time progressed this was becoming more and more important as the technology was growing rapidly from limit switches to complicated electronic controls. Example: the new 1960 rolling mill operation plus electrostatic paint spraying.

During my first week at work, Ken Beck in the production control department came to my office to invite me to the next monthly meeting of the Mirro Management Club. This company-sponsored group was made up of all supervision levels in the manufacturing plants. It was also directly connected and chartered by the "National Management Association". The listing of these levels is worth noting. Starting at the top level of responsibility and listing:

Vice President, Manufacturing
General Plant Manager
Plant Manager
Plant Superintendent
General Foreman
Foreman
Supervisor

Except for the two top spots each of the remaining seemed to have their assistant. This group was also classified as salaried employees versus hourly paid (Also determines status for overtime pay) I became acquainted with a very active group of men and women. To belong, there was a minimal yearly fee and the evening dinner meetings, served at minimal cost. All meetings were well attended, held at several local meeting halls in the area. There was a social hour before dinner and well planned programs to follow. Guest speakers came from many areas of interest, in and outside of the Mirro administration. Presidents and leaders from the area spoke and speakers came from as far away as New York. It was an excellent opportunity for the sales and finance area to present the latest program, products and status of the company. Of course the president was automatically a member and most often present at the meetings.

The first months at Mirro seemed to fly by very rapidly. The monthly meetings of the Management Club were such a great help to me in learning to know all the plant supervision. I heard both their problems and their success stories, and came to know each as an individual. They made me feel at home in one great hurry! Often a plant manager or superintendent would offer a plant tour to the other members or give a short talk on some special project. They seemed to meld as a family and gain from each meeting.

The next challenge I wanted to explore was locating the person in the Finance and Marketing-Sales department areas whose confidence I could win! I had been taught the importance of being in direct contact with both of these key functions. They played such a major part in the make-up and success of any company. Manufacturing was service to these areas; without money and/or customers a firm could not exist. It was also my objective to convince both sales and finance of the obvious fact: the major physical make up of this business was its people and assets to manufacture the very items they had to finance and sell! Without the items there would be no sales to bring in the dollars they had to control or gain! Enough said! We had to be a team to succeed! At this stage, I was not aware what sort of mutual relationship there was between sales and finance and manufacturing. My future success depended on my ability to establish a close and open relationship. I had to gain their respect and confidence.

First on my list was G. C. Kubitz, Senior Vice President and C. W. Ziemer, Vice President of sales-marketing. Meetings were requested and we met over a cup of coffee in the newly remodeled hospitality room, attached to the test kitchen. "Was there any area where they felt the engineering department could be of greater service to them?" This was nothing special to request; after all we had known each other for some time now. Both were active at Branch River Country Club and we often had met for casual conversations, my being a member there for over eleven years. In fact I recall having played golf with them on several occasions. It is quite certain that both had something to do with my coming to work at Mirro. They were certainly aware that both vice presidents of manufacturing were close to retirement. Persons were to be selected soon to be trained as replacements. That is only a supposition on my part but, as I look back now at the casual visits to the F. C. Heiden office by both of them at different times, I realize I was there each time. It seems feasible they were observing my actions as we toured the operations. Recalling some of their questions and comments also point in a positive direction. The meeting ended with both saying they would pass the word on to the total sales group.

The next main meeting was with Mr. L. L. Newberry, Secretary Treasurer. He was known as Mr. Integrity! The name was sure accurate in every respect. I later found out that he was a pillar in the National Baptist Church. He and his wife were wonderful Christian people and a pleasure with whom to spend time. He quickly called in Assistant Treasurer, Uriel Garey: "Ug," as I called him. I had known him from the country club. He had become a regular 4th in our Thursday evening golf outing on stag night. (Ug from Mirro, Thomsen from F.C.Heidens, Tom Gannon and Hank Kollmeyer from Aluminum Specialty Company. We were quite the talk of the Club). As a result of our previous friendship, there developed good relations between our corresponding departments for some time. I really appreciated all the help he gave me in the upcoming months and years.

Located in an office just next to mine was a consultant from Arthur Andersen & Company. Mike Noling had been brought to the Mirro Manufacturing division to develop a Production Planning and Inventory Control System. It was tagged "PPICS". With hindsight, I realize that this was a very important factor in my career with the company. Both Ralph Paddock and Fred Terens had briefed me on this recent program initiation into the company, hoping it would be successful, though the programs were still in question. Seeing that Arthur Andersen & Co. was the auditing firm, I can visualize they were instrumental in their consulting division as employed to help reduce all areas of inventory. Mike was a very intense and active young person--at least 10 years younger than yours truly. (Let's see, in 1965, I was 41 which made him 31) With all the things on my platter to learn and get straight, many hours were spent burning the midnight oil. To my surprise, Mike seemed to be there just as much or even more. Weekends were no exception. I enjoyed his company and now, today, I found out why! He was a graduate ME (All kidding aside, Mike was one great person to know and work with).

CHAPTER 20

"Blessed to Be A Blessing" Could We Be Worthy?

1965

Yes, 1965 was a very busy year for the Thomsen family. Louise, the oldest of our children, was no longer a child but now 15 years old with much activity centered in three places: Lincoln High School, church and home. Nancy, the second in line, and just a year younger, was equally active in the same places. Our boy, Tom, was just turning 13 in June as Mirro Aluminum Company became an important name in the household. They were sure an inspiration to mother and dad. Sunday, as mentioned before, had been named Dad's day (not sure why) but I do know we had many good times doing family things on that day. Early breakfast, then to church for Sunday school was a must. Mother taught, as well as Dad, plus I had Deacon's duties and choir. From early on, be it in Sheboygan, Wisconsin, Chicago, Iron Mountain, Michigan or Manitowoc, Wisconsin, the routine on Sunday did not vary! Dinner was in the oven as the family hurried out the door into a warmed up car. (No room in the small single-car garage, filled with bikes, etc., common to many growing families). Then we returned home well after 12 noon to a good hot dinner or a packed picnic basket, just waiting for a trip to some out-of-town park.

Our church became a source of many close friends. Louise and Egon

IS GOD ON OUR SIDE?

Bohrer had children, Linda and Tim, close in age to our three. The family was also new to First Lutheran Church. We seemed to have much in common and, as a result, became lasting friends. The two Moms helped prepare and serve church dinners, teach Sunday school, teach summer vacation school, plan church picnics, the list goes on and on. Imagine on a New Year's Day, 10 degrees below zero, the nine of us leaving for a hike on the Manitowoc River, five miles west of town. A cooler is filled with roasted chicken, a large thermos of hot chocolate, lots of homemade cookies. The tail gate served as our table when lunch time was near! You had to be close friends to even suggest such an outing without fear of being called insane! They had a summer cottage, and we often joined them there for more good times. Sunday afternoon seemed the natural time for family togetherness.

Add to that our many family trips: The children's first airline trip to Washington D.C., the first rail trip to visit grandparents in Phoenix, Arizona, a visit to the Grand Canyon, a drive to Pasadena for the Rose Parade and Rose Bowl game, many drives to Chicago and staying with grandpa and grandma. Not too sure how this all rated in the kids' minds but to Mom and Dad they were times never to be forgotten. Yes, we were blessed beyond worthiness. Family: what an important part of my life. If I seem to have overlooked much detail of our family togetherness, I have to admit to being a so called workaholic. Dear mother was always there to fill the gap I often left. I'm not proud of it at all, but I don't ever recall using up all the vacation time allowed each year. Not good at all, either for family or myself and, if I had it to do over, I'd spend much more time with family. On the other side of this equation, I can truthfully say that work was a real pleasure and, every morning, I seemed to cherish getting to work. The only exception was my time with Webcor in Chicago. During years at Kohler, Specialty, Heidens, Mirro---many evenings, weekends, even holidays found me at the office or shop. It was an exciting challenge that never ended. Up early, too, I liked to get the paperwork finished before others showed up for work, and then I was off to the plants to talk and listen to happenings of small or large concerns. I desired to have the workers on my side and desired them to know I cared about their well-being. I still had memories of my father visiting regularly on the shop floor when I worked summers at the factory where he was an officer. It played a part in my desire to do the same. The workers then, not knowing he was my Dad, would comment, "There's a guy we respect; he comes around a lot and shows interest in us!"

While work consumed many hours of every week, home was such a pleasure and there were new experiences galore! Some of Mother's letters can best show what I mean. Following are just a few examples.

February 9, 1965.

Hi to all.

Yes, some busy days in January. Dick has had quite a bit of traveling -- having engineering work done in Milwaukee. So once a week, he takes off, leaving at 5:30 a.m., home by supper. Took overnight trip to Los Angeles, drove to Chicago, took plane at midnight, then flew back on Tuesday. So goes his busy schedule.

Busy as he is -- many nights he just throws up his hands and spends time with family -- ice skating together at local rink -- working on mathematical cube model for Louise, helping build a model of Eiffel Tower ; showing Tom how to split wood on the saw -- planning the scale model -- building up with glue and temporary supports. Model stands 4 feet tall -- very impressive and Tom's eyes are dancing. Back to Louise's model -- hollow cube frame with strings, threaded from various sides, looks like Frank Lloyd Wright building creation.

Tom and Dick have been planning their model railroad -- working as they can on drawings. Dick helping Louise with tricky algebra problems, he likes the challenge. 1st question that the children ask as he comes in, "Busy tonight"? Busy or not -- always seems to find an hour before going back to work, relaxing with them on one of their problems.

Louise spent the past 2 weeks -- 1½ hours after school each day -- learning to operate and understand a small Univac computer, owned by the high school. Extremely interested -- spent many hours pounding the books at home. There are 5 children from math club, working together. Along with this study, school staged a career day at which time they were able to sit in on 2 different sessions about their chosen career. Local men and women came to speak on their profession. Louise was bursting with pride, as her father was speaking for the engineering profession. Louise at the present time is interested in programming computers and has done much research on her term paper. Mathematics seems to be a challenge she wants in her profession.

Wish I could have shared the twinkle in Tom's eye as he tried to cover up his extreme pride in having won 1st chair in the Coronet section of the beginners' band. All the world was dancing! Nancy bursting with delight over a 100 math paper –"A" in home economics and the same on the sewing machine test. Working at home with scraps of material on doll clothes. Nancy turned junior high Gal!, she consented to let me trim her hair and Louise worked out a new style for her -- with all the compliments in school yesterday, didn't think she could live with herself -- bursting with self-pride -- half the time spent looking at herself in the mirror.

Dick and the kids playing duets on the piano and organ -- such a treat to my ear. I so enjoy all that practicing, knowing they are having fun and doing what they like. The last weekend of January we all went up to the Bohrer's cottage and spent the afternoon ice skating on the lake and hiking through their woods. Back to their home later for evening around the fireplace with barbecue and goodies. Such a fun and relaxing day together.

Greetings from all of us, Eli.

May 24, 1965.

Hello to all.

Tom and I finished up our 25 mile bike ride Saturday. Last of his cycle badge requirements. He is the 1st Manitowoc boy in at least 8 years to earn the badge and his counselor has never had anyone complete this badge before. We shared a lot of good times biking together -- good fellowship for bonding together. Our friendship, "mom & son", started out at 6:30 a.m. on the way to Two Rivers. There was a beautiful sun, lighting up the sky before sunrise, with the brilliant hues of pink and red -- then there was that same sun coming out of the water like a fluorescent ball -- growing more brilliant as it moved into the sky until I could no longer look -- an electrifying experience -- almost unbelievable. God is dead? How could He be? Had to be a God to plan it and create all of this. The experience of that sunrise will leave a deep memory of trust and security in our God for us.

Big news! Louise passed her driving test! What a day -- fog, misty -- dark out at 9 a.m., streets wet from rain all night and as we entered the courthouse -- 2 friends left saying they had flunked out on their test. Nice way to start. But Louise had her emotional experience before and was very relaxed. All went well.

Bushels of love to all, Eli.

IS GOD ON OUR SIDE?

November 9, 1965.

Hello from Manitowoc.

Winter is coming, 29°, crisp air has brought lovely clear and bright blue skies with sun streaming in the window. We decided to have the family room carpet cleaned. Of course we had to move all the furniture out of the room first. Decided to have ourselves a dance session, while the room was so empty. Louise mentioned social dancing in the gym class at school, having trouble with the fox trot! On went the record player and Dick proceeded to help her out. Where's the record player? in the living room. It had to be mighty loud to hear it in the family room -- this was a jumping household. Tom nearly dropped his "teeth" to see his father's hidden talent of dancing -- us old fogies, dancing! Couldn't believe it! Next day Nancy announced she was going to the 8th grade dance at junior high; all the after effects? Guess she decided it could be fun. At one point, Dick said to turn on some jitterbug music and "lead footed mother" proceeded to try and be his partner. Show the kids how it was done in our day. What a laugh! Biggest joke -- father's legs next morning, "not so good".

Nancy got moved up a chair in A band -- met the challenge, she was so pleased. Louise will be playing the piano in church for both services this Sunday. Very pleased they take an interest in music. Dick will be in Chicago next Monday for seminar meetings. He has been much more active in SAM -- (Society for Advancement of Management) -- and now attends monthly meetings of the Professional Engineers. Each month, Mirro Company has a dinner meeting for management in the manufacturing division. With all of this going on, it sure fills our calendar in a hurry.

Love to all, Eli

"BLESSED TO BE A BLESSING" COULD WE BE WORTHY?

Lesson #8

Yes, Eli and I had been blessed many times over! It was our duty and privilege to be a blessing! We continued to ask for His help!

CHAPTER 21

Time To Stop Listening--
Time to Plan and Take Charge!

1966

The year was 1966. On July 22, just a year after joining Mirro, production workers began an 80-day strike! This was devastating to both employees and their families, to the company, the community and our customers. I left Kohler because of similar conditions. This was very disturbing to me. Had I made a poor choice in joining a firm that could not gain common ground with their long-time employees? I recalled the conversations with Ralph Paddock during the early days at Mirro. He was concerned that the history of the company reflected frequent work stoppages that disrupted production, plus hurt everyone concerned.

As a result of this 80-day work stoppage, sales dropped in 1966 from 59.2 million in '65 to 47.4 million, nearly 20% down and with earnings per share dropping 52%. It was not a good year for Mirro! However, plant expansion programs that had been in progress when I came were completed on schedule. Both plants in Two Rivers (#1 & #4) had multi-story additions; the Boat Plant in Manitowoc had a sizable square footage added and the Rolling Mill large addition including a large grinding machine for Mill Roll finishing. Total plant space now exceeded 2.3 million square feet, a lot of area to maintain,

◄ IS GOD ON OUR SIDE?

pay the utilities and taxes! It led me to spend hours thinking about my future and the company's. My mother had always said I was a dreamer! She wondered if it was a case of being lazy, sleepy or just plain "don't bother me." At this time I was hoping and dreaming that somehow this distrust of workers, the increased overhead costs, and lack of togetherness could be changed. I hoped for a change in which labor and management could see each other as partners, each interested in growth and success to the benefit of all. Little did I realize that I would be involved in that relationship in a very short period of time.

Albert L. Vits had retired as President, remaining as Chairman of the Board. Mr. C. W Ziemer moved from Senior V.P of Marketing/Sales to President and CEO. But not all was doom and gloom for the year. The Metal Cookware Industry forecasts indicated a 10% increase in demand for our products in the coming year. Mirro became licensed to apply the new Teflon coating process developed by the Boeing Company and the engineers were successful in the installation of electrostatic application of coating. This process proved to be a large cost savings in the use of the expensive Teflon materials. A lot of credit goes to Elmer Torke, in charge of research engineering, spear heading this important project.

Along with all my new responsibilities, the rather huge facilities and co-workers surrounding this 42-year- old engineer, a Manitowoc business friend had recommended to the city council that I replace him on the Public Utilities Commission. This person happened to be president of the Manitowoc Company. We first met at a meeting of SAM (Society for Advancement of Management). The Utility appointment lasted for 15 years. It not only proved to be very interesting working with other business people, including the Major, but a tremendous education in civil affairs, politics, electric generation/distribution and water procurement/purification. We met monthly at the City Hall, many meetings lasting into dinner time cutting time spent with family in the evenings.

TIME TO STOP LISTENING--TIME TO PLAN AND TAKE CHARGE!

By year's end, I was beginning to feel at home at Mirro. Time was flitting by much too fast---so many things to learn and to plan for. Evenings at the office were spent trying to evaluate when to stop listening and absorbing the surroundings and start planning my own future actions. Up to this point it was evident I was putting out fires, trying to help my managers in engineering solve their problems and answering sales/marketing, finance, and the presidential questions. Contract sales was absorbing big chunks of my time. This included work for the auto industry, questions from Sears, Kelvinator, Hot Point, May Tag, and on and on. While new and challenging issues were involved, this is not what I knew I was hired for by Mr. Vits. Thus a shift in gears on my part was attempted.

When working at Aluminum Specialty, many hours were spent on the golf course, at lunch, in evening get-togethers and business trips with my good friends, Tom Gannon & Hank Kohlmeyer. The subject of competitor, Mirro, became a favorite subject. I was the "young kid" in the group and my ears were well tuned to the output of these two men, gifted with such great experience! All kidding aside, we three seemed to hit it off well together; I was the youngest by nearly ten years and appreciated their willingness to accept me as part of their business world. Passing comments often led to how top-heavy Mirro management appeared. This resulted in an inability to make quick decisions and rather obsolete ways of doing business. This made Mirro big, slow, and cumbersome at times.

After my first year at this "Big Mirro," yes, I could see it in my area of responsibility and in the manufacturing division! I had also learned that to be heard and to be effective as a manager, it was required to plan ahead, to be alert to the needs of my counterparts, while gaining their respect. Simultaneously, I had to delegate to those who showed the capability to perform. The latter gave me the time to plan other matters better, thus becoming more consistent in my actions. Not all of this wisdom came to me out of the blue and by experience! To my great surprise, one afternoon Fred Terens (Sr.VP, Manufacturing) called me into his office and told me I had been recommended for attending a month of information training in New York City. It was presented by the NMA (Nation Management Association) Attendance required one week at a time over a 6-month period. It was very interesting and loaded with great managing information including presentations by outstanding business leaders. Computer technology was just beginning to explode in the manufacturing world. Software to facilitate simulation of operating make-believe companies was used and it proved enlightening as well as very informative. Hours were spent with other attendees (business persons of all ages and background--- some from Europe and Asia) solving everyday problems that were presented by the leaders.

My past experience, plus this very current off campus training, gave me new insight. I felt even more confident in revolving to a planning mode. Could I play a part in the future of this company called Mirro. Mr. Terens presented me with this training opportunity. Then he sent another message to me. When we met, he asked me some very rather unusual questions in the guise of asking for suggestions. "What would I do if in his position or if such and such happened?" Or "If so-and-so retired who do you think could step into that position?" At the end of our conversation he suggested we get together after returning from the New York sessions and continue the conversation.

This presented the real push for me to evaluate my work plans for the future. Looking back now, I realize how naive I was. It is obvious to me now, Wes Day (consultant), Ally Vits and Fred Terens were all suggesting possible potential for me to progress up in the management ranks if and when I met their requirements and did the "right" things without upsetting any apple carts on the way! I had learned to "be alert to the needs of my counterparts and gain their respect." This was so important and it paid off for me, Mr. Ziemer became the new CEO! We had close contact in the work with Arthur Andersen &Company in developing a working/planning tool combining the PPICS system with a computer marketing forecasting program. So it was that I began spending those evening hours planning the best I could. My engineering team was extremely helpful and more than

TIME TO STOP LISTENING--TIME TO PLAN AND TAKE CHARGE!

willing to accept responsibility; they had the experience to make good calls, I only asked that they keep me informed.

As Mr. Ziemer took on his new responsibilities as president and A.L. Vits moved to Chairman of the Board, big changes were made in the sales area! Frank Prescott moved to VP Sales, Frank Timberlake was promoted to General Sales Manager, and Richard Stolz, to Assistant General Sales Manager. I had become very familiar with each of them and it was great to see them move up. In 1966 they had invited me to attend the large housewares show conducted at Chicago's McCormick Place. The experience was not new to me; I had attended several times while at Aluminum Specialty. It did allow me to meet and develop good relations with the many salesmen and representatives for the company. Meeting with the many customers was also a plus. From then on, each year it became a privilege to attend this National Sales Show. It certainly gave me a much broader view of the total industry, an opportunity to meet and talk with my counterparts in other companies as well as key suppliers.

It was in this year of 1966 that we as a family took a most welcome vacation trip to Washington D.C. It was the first airline trip for the children and what a wonderful time we had! We stayed at a motel just across the river from the soon-to-be-famous Watergate Motel. We met our Congressman from Wisconsin, and we toured the city from one end to the other. The best food was found in the Art Museum. There was some really "high tech" stuff in the Art Museum. For a small fee you could obtain a hand held voice-emitting device that gave you history and explanation of the painting in front of you. Wow! That was a big deal then. We rented a car while there and were able to visit "history" and see for ourselves the many documents that made possible this wonderful country we live in.

Another happening in this particular summer of '66 was the expenditure for a used, tandem balloon-tired Schwinn bicycle. I'm not sure who used it the most but it always seemed in demand. I recall the story of mother saying she witnessed our Tom tossing a watermelon

IS GOD ON OUR SIDE?

Louise and Nancy on the Tandem!

back and forth to his friend, Jim, while coasting down the N 12th Street hill. That takes terrific "guts" or balance and technique (or something!) The task of remodeling the girls' bedroom was also undertaken. It included a dropped ceiling, new vanity, big mirror, wall papering and painting, with new carpeting and wall hangings of their choice. These events provided good diversity for me, with all that was going on at Mirro. After Grandpa Zapel passed away in August, the house seemed a bit empty to us all.

Several of Eli's letters give a feel as to the activities at home.

February 23, 1966.

Hi, Ho, to all!

Have to share with you all the joy for happenings of the past week -- music, music, music! It's been lovely.

TIME TO STOP LISTENING--TIME TO PLAN AND TAKE CHARGE! ➤

Last Thursday, the concert band at Junior high gave their 1st concert for the parents. To see those 125 youngsters in their brilliant uniforms up on stage gives a surge of pride in itself. To know "your own" are involved! Bright orange blazers and black pants. Director chose so many fine selections -- kids had a great time playing -- they so enjoy working with him. The light side of the concert was excerpts from My Fair Lady.

During last week at the annual Youth Music Recital, Sunday afternoon, the big day -- Louise played brilliantly -- played better than Dick and I have ever heard her. As Mel Kitzerow (teacher), said -- "she shines when she is "on" and is cool as a cucumber". Seems to get lost in the piano and puts so much into what she is playing. Great for us to view, the Louise we didn't know.--more accomplished at playing than we would hear at practice time. What a proud day.

Tom camped out with the Boy Scouts over the weekend. Left Friday after school -- got back Sunday noon -- cold, hungry and very tired. Naturally, no sleep! -- And the temperatures at 15 below those nights -- they really roughed it. He ate up all the food here in sight -- took a long bath and crawled into bed for a nap. From all reports, the boys had a great time. Ice fishing, sledding and skating -- good to be on their own.

Nancy had such fun making up table decorations for our Valentine table. Just a special reason for having a special family dinner together. She and Tom purchased heart shaped suckers from local candy shop, and what whoppers they were, had them wrapped each separately and so attractively decorated -- much work by both to make it a very special day for all. We all laughed at Dick's box of candy for me -- "that's his dessert after meals" -- always wants that piece of candy, takes after his "Pappy".

Well, that's us, full of activity. All is well here, having

IS GOD ON OUR SIDE?

wonderful days; Love Eli

June 14, 1966.

What excitement. Start of Bible school yesterday -- 148 children in attendance -- have 20 teachers, and almost that many helpers involved, big production. Again, I am co-director this year. Indications are that I may become the director in the future.

Louise left last Saturday morning, 7 AM, by bus to Ely, Minnesota -- 600 miles north -- 11 hour ride -- 21 girls from senior scout troop, on a canoe trip. Going into Canada. They will arrive home late Saturday night, cost was $30 including all equipment and food -- only brought small bag with personal supplies. Bus transportation, $11.50 round-trip -- so reasonable a trip for her.

On the 27th, we will fly to Washington, D.C. for our family vacation will be staying at the Howard Johnson motel West of the White House on the Potomac River. Swimming pool on the roof, found the cheapest rates here for the family of 5 and can accommodate us all in one room. Also making reservations in Williamsburg, Pennsylvania and to stay overnight. So we can view that area. So excited -- a real vacation trip and chance to fly. Plus chance to get educated around the history of our great America -- we're bursting!

Busy sewing clothes -- don't have that many hot weather clothes in this part of the country -- don't need them here, so make easy fitting shifts and will be set for the trip. I'm off to bed -- good to share all things with you. Happy July vacation to you too -- and do hope Dad's coming won't delay any plans you might have for this month of your own.

Best love from us all, Eli

TIME TO STOP LISTENING--TIME TO PLAN AND TAKE CHARGE!

July 27, 1966

School comes all too soon. That word, "school" is a nasty word today -- we want to live up to the fullest before Labor Day. With many prescheduled things for summer, time slipped quickly. Louise finished up her driver education course at vocational school -- behind the wheel -- then takes her road test at age 16 for her permanent driver's license. Growing up too fast!

Nancy busy 3 mornings babysitting and then is busy baking for me -- Tom working on his Boy Scout ProDeato award and giving service time to church. Keeps mother busy keeping them all on schedule. Gave up on the canning and doing sewing -- too many interruptions. Not like it used to be but love it.

Will keep you posted on Dad's (Zapel) condition, pleased with his progress, he is glad for the good care he is getting.

Best love, Eli

October 4, 1966.

Manty News Bulletin!

Since Dad's (Zapel) passing in August, there seems to be so much happening and going on at our house. Louise seems to be going in circles, so many activities. Has joined the AFS club -- Art club -- math club and is now working out for swim club. She was elected treasurer of the Luther League at church, still with piano lessons, Girl Scouts, working on junior float for her homecoming parade, many nights of great fun, tried to "sandwich" in some sewing, but time is short.

Nancy has piano lessons on Tuesday, choir on Wednesday, and confirmation of Saturday mornings. This plus activity at school, scouts on Monday night, and swim club on Tuesday. Tom still has Boy Scouts, confirmation on Wednesday and choir on Thursday.

Dick is back in full swing with the Bethel Bible teacher's class every Monday night. My Bethel Bible study student course starts this coming Wednesday. Dick joined the choir again -- so enjoys it -- but already it looks as though Wednesday nights will be getting busy. Hope he can continue to go to choir practice, and guess what; I again have my 5th grade Sunday school class. Tom working yet on his bike badge. Has finished his 6, 25 mile hikes, I took the last round with him. PTA starts again, this year Dick is president of junior high PTA. Add to all this plus work and now has been elected to the City Public Utility Commission for a 5 year term, meeting twice each month.

My biggest job is just keeping the family organized -- all go such separate ways in the day and at night -- I've decided I'll just be the cog around which the wheel turns or nothing would be stable in this foundation! Cartoon picture of me would show eye on the clock and on the calendar, mind on reminding family of this or that and part-time chauffeur. What fun!

Time for the postman -- already delayed this too long -- so off it goes. Happiness to all,

Much love, Eli.

October 4, 1966.

Is your day as bright and lovely as ours? Just great being

TIME TO STOP LISTENING--TIME TO PLAN AND TAKE CHARGE!

alive and enjoying this beautiful world. Yes. Fall is my favorite season, and the hues of the trees, the crisp--cool air, the crunch of leaves, the harvest Moon -- and the sunny days --, wow, this is the season to just soak the eyeballs and fill the spirit for the winter. If today could be busier for Dick, don't know how! He had 6 meetings scheduled for tonight -- Professional Engineering meeting took 1st preference. He is program chairman for the Fox River Valley group tonight. The whole week has been a wild one for him. Yesterday, left at 5:45 AM for Milwaukee. Not home until late, so goes it -- about all we see of him is to say "Hi".

Much love to all, Eli

CHAPTER 22

Promotion to General Manager of Manufacturing Engineering--"Plant Production!"

By the end of 1966, the manufacturing Production Planning and Inventory Control system was in full use. Mike Noling of Arthur Andersen & Company was involved with the marketing/sales groups, installing a forecasting system for both long range and yearly updates. These two programs were then tied together, thus enabling us to plan joint equipment and labor needs for each of the operating plants! A lot of credit must be given to these new computer systems for the improvement in company efficiency and in customer service. They certainly were made to order for me to improve my thinking and planning for the future. Forecasting of sales became the key to how the company was to grow and how profits could be retained for the growth. In July of 1967, just two years after my arrival, I was given the new title of General Manager of Manufacturing Engineering. The added responsibility now included production, planning & control".

The forecasts developed by the sales groups spelled out by item what and when the customers would order and in what quantity. This was no small task, considering the thousands of items in our product line. These figures were then placed into the manufacturing computer system, giving us estimated hours of work for each and every production center in each individual plant. What a wonderful planning tool! It was a tool to place equal responsibility on both sales and manufacturing to stick their neck out in regard to what they were going to sell and manufacturing thus became committed to produce the requested supply on time. If we could not meet their forecast, we had to state why--- be it lack of material, equipment, space or labor. They, in turn, could then revise their plan till we could meet their requirements. It was essentially a two-way street that provided teamwork between the two divisions! The third part to the team planning was the finance group. They now had a better way of knowing what type of cash flow or financing would be required and when. New equipment would have to be purchased, or the plant expanded, and how much material would be purchased and when. It sounds very simplistic but it took many hours of trial and error, meetings galore, and fine tuning by many of us. It was well into 1967 and 1968 before we began to feel comfortable in the process, learning to have confidence in each other and the reliability of the computer programs to furnish us timely information. It was very exciting for me, as I now had moved into a new and welcome area encompassing the production of product as well as the planning the facility to do the production.

This new responsibility stimulated the need for increased planning of my own future and how the Company could meet the growth being forecast by the Salespeople. My office was just a few doors north of the Personnel Managers. Ed Reed and staff were frequently contacted as we discussed trends regarding available workers in each area. Could this region supply the labor force in the future? My monthly meeting with the Manitowoc Public Utilities commission, which included the City Mayor, was giving me knowledge regarding area population and its growth. This was all new territory for me and it presented a challenge. Could I make a long range projection of what labor force would be required during each of the next 40 years? I decided to give it a try, using historical data that seemed easily available from the library, the Public Utilities, and Mirro employment records. It turned out to be a much longer and time consuming project than I ever imagined. I'll leave the total story of that

PROMOTION TO GENERAL MANAGER OF MANUFACTURING ENGINEERING--"PLANT PRODUCTION!"

project for later in this writing.

Along with my planning at work, much was taking place at home. The kids and Eli were just as busy, if not even more so!

> *February 2 & 25, 1967.*
>
> *Golly, it's fun with teenagers -- always surprises in life, fun things to share.*
>
> *On January 20 we took Tom to Milwaukee where he finally was able to purchase his dream of a "ham radio" receiving set. Cannot send or get license for sending until he is 18, but he can receive and listen to people all over the world. Dick helped the following Sunday to string copper wire for the aerial. All around and through the attic, drilled holes in the bedroom wall for connection downstairs. They had a happy afternoon sharing new experiences, and the joy of the 1st broadcast was heard. Gals and I spent the day sewing -- everything was humming on the 2nd floor.*
>
> *Newest measurements of all 3.*
>
> > *Louise- 5'9" 133 lb..*
> >
> > *Nancy-5'7 ¼" 119 lb. (year ago 131# 5'6 ¾")*
> >
> > *Tom 5'11 ¼" 140lb (year ago 126# 5'7 ½")*
>
> *When we were in Milwaukee with Tom, we had lunch at Mader's, what a treat with all that good German food. Dick has been involved for many Sundays now at church preparing for the Billy Graham movie crusade here in Manitowoc. The movie will be followed by discussions at church with our pastor.*

IS GOD ON OUR SIDE?

Here it is 25 February! Where is everyone now? Well, Nancy is at confirmation -- Tom working at church, dusting, running sweeper, waxing floors. Dick is at the office -- just difficult to keep up with all the meetings required during the daytime hours -- only evenings and weekends to do his own work. As a new challenge, scheduling and organizing production, with sales. Besides this he now still has 3 weeks left of schooling in New York -- Bethel teachers' classes -- we all put in our appointments to see him. Louise -- this weekend is off touring the Lutheran colleges with Pastor. Last night, Tom and Nancy were at the Valentine dance at junior high. How interesting to talk with Tom later and get the dating news from the boy's point of view -- he's most anxious to confide in me -- I hold that in high honor.

Since I last wrote, pastor again scheduling Lenten luncheon for men at the church. Each Monday meet at 12 o'clock for food for the body and soul. Then Bible study to follow. Dick finds them most stimulating and great to share with other men of the congregation, I help serve the lunch.

Last Saturday we got to watch Tom play basketball. Final game of the season. It was played at the Lincoln high school gym -- big-time stuff on that huge floor. Nancy's club had a bake sale to raise funds for cheerleaders, really great when daughter has these bake sales, we all participate in eating some in the evening! Nancy at present thinking of veterinarian work, airline stewardess, or being a kindergarten teacher. My, such interesting conversations around this house lately. Louise has spent 1 ½ weeks writing applications for the summer program of the National Science Foundation. Tom mentioned, something I thought he had only sketchily thought of a year or so ago but still on his mind. "Maybe you'll laugh, but I'm still thinking about being a minister." Laugh, no, told him he would have the greatest product in the world to sell!

Happiness to you all! Eli

March 21 & 29, 1967.

Sunday the 19th was Nancy's time to shine. She played the offertory solo at both services. Mr. Kitzerow accompanied her on the Organ -- all went very well. She came home singing as she came in the door! Her self-confidence grew 100% -- she did it! She did it! She was the most pleased gal in the world! As a treat, we all went to Fox Hills for Sunday dinner. For Easter Sunday, Louise and Nancy's Chapel choir sang all 3 services. Tom's Carol choir along with Dad's Senior choir ending with the Hallelujah chorus! Sent chills down my spine!

Love to all, Eli

Thursday, May 11, 1967

Believe the height of emotion came last Tuesday when Louise got a call that she was accepted at the Walla Walla Washington. Literally shook and sobbed and smiled, just unbelievable. This was for the National Science Foundation summer school program.

On the 21st. Nancy will be confirmed -- this is the big event of our next week. And we certainly don't want anything to interfere. So added together, then almost too exciting around here -- most wonderful too. One Saturday Dad took us to Milwaukee, and we found a confirmation dress for Nancy -- flower girl dress for Louise and Dick found a summer suit, all at Marshall Field's. We got to travel in our new Buick.

IS GOD ON OUR SIDE?

Tom has been having a great time with his math teacher after school hours. They are working together on antiques. Going to auctions, meeting to redo things, new friend for both. Is finishing up an old tread sewing machine for a desk -- bit too small for him -- but fun in doing. Glad he has a hobby, where he is using his hands.

Much love, Eli

CHAPTER 23

Manitowoc Paper "New Vice President and Director of Mirro"

1967-68

July 16, 1967.

Greetings.

Exciting news -- can't contain ourselves -- bursting our buttons -- so proud of our daddy -- so thrilled. He can be so recognized, given such responsibility and challenge, the Lord has blessed us abundantly. Dick is promoted to vice president. He now reports to Mr. Fred Terens, senior vice president of manufacturing, who retires in 2 years. The possibilities are unlimited. He can only strive to prove himself worthy and capable. Lots of hard work -- long hours -- before him.

Eli.

◄ IS GOD ON OUR SIDE?

August 3, 1967

Big News

Dick had two very busy weeks; annual sales conferences here at the home office. Asked to give speech plus attend meetings. So no time for regular work. Best part and compliment paid to him after his talk (which was the closing one for the week's conference, touchy spot to be in -- leaves them "high" or "flat". Pres. Ziemer mentioned that all the men had nicknames -- Dick too new to have acquired a handle yet -- but after listening to his speech at the end of the 2nd week they knew there were only 2 choices. "Rev. Thomsen or Billy Graham". Had tears in my eyes for the honor it meant today. He could be both a Christian and a businessman -- an evangelist in his work and respected for it. That was the highest compliment, and worth more than any "raise". Made me so happy he's mine! See, 20 years! Just makes it even more wonderful together -- yes. That's the number next Wednesday, where did those 20 years go?

Much love, Eli

In February, 1968, Mr. Paddock retired. He'd been such a wonderful help to me; his departure was one that I had hoped would not take place for a long time. However, it was no great surprise; I had been told of this possible eventuality even before I was brought on board at Mirro. What did surprise me was when Fred Terens (Sr. VP, Manufacturing) called me into his office and said I should move into the office vacated by Mr. Paddock. It was just next to Mr. Terens. The following day he was giving me lots of work to look at and asking me my advice on some organizational problems. Most all of the questions raised pertained to the future.

MANITOWOC PAPER "NEW VICE PRESIDENT AND DIRECTOR OF MIRRO"

Sales were still suffering from the 80-day strike of 1966 with an increase in '67 of only 6%. All indications were that '68 would still not surpass the level reached before the strike. One of Mr. Paddock's last requests was: "Dick, do all you can to prevent another work stoppage in the future; it hurts everyone!" Only two months later, the 1st Qtr Board of Directors met in Pittsburgh, and appointed Richard Thomsen, Vice President Manufacturing and new member of the Board of Directors. It was also announced that Mr. Terens would retire at year's end. I could now understand all the work and questions Mr. Terens had thrown my way.

With my new title came the responsibilities for personnel (today called human relations), labor negotiations, purchasing, material control and inventory control. This coupled with my present title of Production Planning Controller; put me in a position of determining all of the plants' scheduling and operations. This was a huge responsibility that I had not dreamed could take place this quickly. Along with these announcements came the retirement of Mr. C.G. McGlynn, Manager of Purchasing and the appointment of Bob Franz as his replacement. Bob had been well trained in the function and was a pleasure to work with. Yes, 1968 was a real whirlwind of a year for me. For this, I owe so much to others, including my family that was so willing to permit me the time. They had great patience with me. I would rush home, grab a few hours with them, and then hurry back to burn the midnight oil at the office (Thank you, my dear family!)

A little interesting sidelight to my experiences. Mr. Newberry was not a person who felt comfortable using the airlines. Therefore, Director Meetings held in New Jersey or Pittsburgh involved a lengthy train ride for him. My being the junior member of the board qualified me as the candidate to keep him company. It was actually a real pleasure, a chance to relax and to get to know Mr. Newberry as a Christian friend and a very knowledgeable expert in the history of the Mirro Company. Learning the function and responsibilities of board members was all new to me. What an excellent opportunity to ask and be educated in that respect! He was patient, understanding, and behaved like a father to me. On that first trip, he told me in confidence his plans for retirement in the not- too-distant future. The pattern continued in my receiving these unexplained opportunities. It was in this way that the Secretary Treasurer of Mirro for so many years became my friend and mentor. In such a fashion, I was the recipient of almost unlimited hours of uninterrupted conversation. I'm sure many of my questions would have appeared childish to the normal business executive, but not to Mr. Newberry. He appeared only excited, stating over and over how all our conversation would be kept in confidence---no question too trivial or insignificant. He was anxious for me to be successful. On our return rail trip the conversation would continue, ending with both relating their experience and love of the church. I hope I was in some small way able to meet his standards and expectations. I was to miss this fine man acutely in the future!

The economy in the Manitowoc area was doing very well and the labor market was becoming very tight. It was becoming difficult for all industries to procure workers. The new computer forecasting and production planning system was now very usable. It was evident that Manufacturing had to develop a new source of manpower to meet the needs of our sales. Again by chance, it was brought to our attention that an apparel company from out East was closing its manufacturing plant in the town of Gillett, Wisconsin. The town fathers were actively searching for some light industry to fill this rather new and clean facility. Upon visiting and meeting with city officials, we found an area of surplus labor and a facility that was ideal for electric appliance assembly operations. There was 24,000 square feet on one level floor space, rail and truck docking. An agreement was reached, plans were set in motion, and the facility was acquired. To add to the work of the plant engineers, machinery had to be moved, plus over 50,000 square Feet were added to the building. It was a new undertaking for many of us in the engineering area. I was thankful again for the experience received in my work at Aluminum Specialty, setting up the shell plant in Iron Mountain, Michigan. Management

MANITOWOC PAPER "NEW VICE PRESIDENT AND DIRECTOR OF MIRRO"

Corn Poppers To Gillett, WI

personnel had to be selected, office arranged and equipped, product line selected, utilities arranged for, machinery selected and installed, local contractors arranged and Critical Path programs developed to allow for continual customer supply of whatever products were to be moved to the new plant.

So it was in 1968 that the responsibility for labor negotiations fell into my lap as well. The labor contracts signed in mid-1966 were to end in mid-1969. Little breathing room was given to me for preparations of this upcoming event. The company negotiating team was now made up of Ed Read (Personnel Director), Al Drobka (Mgr. Industrial Engineer) and yours truly. Keep in mind, talks with the Union leaders began months before contract's end. We were starting to regain full production since the last disastrous walk out, and the challenge of Mr. Paddock to find a solution to better relations with employees remained strong in my mind. So with all the other happenings in the year, there was little time to dream; actions had to take place simultaneously. There were many meetings to attend with my group of managers,. In addition, I had to visit all plants on a regular basis and hold meetings with my counterparts in sales and finance. How fortunate to have such a talented and capable group of managers reporting to me. They were outstanding!

IS GOD ON OUR SIDE?

If you recall my conversations with Mr. Vits at my hiring interview. At that meeting, I stated my full intentions to visit all plants, and to meet the workers so they knew who I was. I did not intend to spend all of my time on the 7th floor office territory. The people on the production floor knew where the problems were and in most cases could offer the best approach to finding answers. Also recall my youthful experience while working in my father's factory. His people liked and respected him because he knew and listened to them! This promise had been kept in my first two years at Mirro. I had specifically gone out of my way to meet, converse with, and get to know the Union presidents wherever they were, plus as many other workers as time would permit.

In the initial meetings with the Steel Workers' Union, it was rather difficult for me. Often old sores were opened, and there was vulgar language and yelling. For the company team, we had agreed that Ed Reed would be our only spokesman. He was excellent and kept his cool much better than I could have done. In past years he had also been the spokesperson and no officer of the company ever attended the negotiation meetings. For me to be there not only broke tradition but placed me in a rather dangerous position. If I were to make a commitment to the Union, it would have been impossible to retract it without a grievous loss of faith in our position. In the past, Ed could always say he had to receive approval from his superior on any subject before agreement could be reached. For that reason I very seldom said anything! However, after a few outbursts, I voiced a firm objection to any swearing and vulgarity and made it clear to all that it would not be tolerated.

Pages of notes were taken by the three of us. After meetings, we would compare notes and make plans for the next one. The meetings were all conducted after working hours. The Union participants would come after their work shift. Meetings were held weekly as a rule, beginning in the early part of the year, extending over months. Also keep in mind that there were four different unions with which we had to negotiate and in separate meetings. Because the union representing the production works included the majority of employees, the Craft Workers Union (machinists & electricians) usually accepted the same form and content. Enough said about this subject; to cover all the details and time spent would consume several books this size. I will simply say the meetings became very businesslike and ended up being meaningful. A 3-year contract was signed with the production workers; a 1-year Contract with the machinists & electricians; a 2-year contract with the workers in "Plant A" (Aluminum House Siding was produced at this operation in Southern Wisconsin).

In my fifteen years of direct responsibility for labor negotiations, not one strike or work stoppage occurred. I feel my regular visits to the plants constituted a direct reason. Could it be that they, too, said, "There's a guy we respect?" Only they can answer that. A lot of wonderful, loyal, and hardworking people worked at Mirro. Generation after generation, families continued to work at our many plants. An effort was made to visit every one of those plants each month. It was

My Office as Vice President & Director of Mirro

a privilege to work with them---a true privilege.

A little sidelight: In April it was possible for me to meet my brother, Jack, in Chicago and the two of us flew to Arizona for my parents' 50th Wedding Anniversary. What a wonderful trip!

March 19, 1968

Our big news -- Louise received honor scholarship at Luther College! --- so proud of our Louise; she's intelligent - but not a brain -- has had to work very hard for her grades! Tom came home that same day to announce the band members at school had elected him. Mr. Band for this quarter. He really beamed! Nancy is taking driver education at school -- -- behind the wheel training will be this summer -- -- they do grow up!

What a terrific weekend with the Luther College Band performance! We had 4 girls with us overnight -- most enjoyable for us and for Louise -- she asked question after question. One gal flautist, so much in appearance as our Nancy, and one gal had percussion, and then bassoon player and a Coronet player. After church shared Sunday dinner.

All our love, Eli.

May 13, 1968.

So much to say, big news! Richard N. Thomsen -- VP, Mirro Aluminum Company

Wow! -- There we cried and pinched ourselves and we are so humble -- just can't be -- but it is -- just have a huge task

MANITOWOC PAPER "NEW VICE PRESIDENT AND DIRECTOR OF MIRRO"

to now prove himself worthy of the title. Never in the wildest dreams did we think this could come true. Now Dick's immediate boss, Mr. Terens, Senior VP -- retires in November, what does the future hold in store?

Then Saturday, Tom won an A rating at the citywide music Festival for his coronet playing-- -- tears and more tears of joy -- -- he has worked so hard, he is so proud!

With this, however, comes most tragic news -- -- on Monday evening, 3 senior girls, one a very close friend of Louise, were killed in a car accident, 2 others still in the hospital. The town was shocked! Lea Ann, her friend, one who gave her a corsage for going away to college last summer. She was in the church choir with Louise, lived a block from here. Her mom asked some of her choir friends to sing for the funeral. The Holy Spirit answered our prayers and upheld those 3 girls as they sang Children of the Heavenly Father and Beautiful Savior.

Not sure when Dick will eat today. Meetings all day at work, public utilities commission meeting at 5 PM -- Bethel Bible classes at 6:30 and 7:30 -- choir practice, following at 8:30 -- we are together in the spirit, but not often in presence, Ha!

Our love in heaps, Eli

CHAPTER 24

Prayer Makes A Difference!

So what has all this got to do with the question: Is God On Our Side? What made me decide to write a book that many might read, and not just a family history? What did my career have to do with God being on my side, or with God being on our nation's side, or your side or my side? I would like to devote this chapter, a short break in the life of 3W, with the intent of conveying why I feel it so important to show how lives can teeter on an edge---an edge determined by decisions that can affect the outcome of our lives, either for the good, for better, or for best. God forbid that the outcome of our lives be for the worst.

This interruption in my personal life story was chosen for a purpose. This "young engineer" as I have often called myself up this point, had basically been on the move upward at a rather rapid and consistent rate! Was I, of all people, somehow forever-blessed---so much on God's side that nothing negative could ever happen to "Dick Thomsen"? To the contrary. At the beginning of this book it was stated that one intent was to fulfill the requests of my family to write a summary of my business career. Like a good engineer, an outline was the starting point in establishing my content. I consulted photo albums, newspaper clippings, check books, school yearbooks, company reports, letters, every little tidbit I could find to fill in each year of my life. As I researched, I realized that the years 1967-8 constituted a landmark---a point at which a light began to shine upon

◂ IS GOD ON OUR SIDE?

a common thread running and working its way through the lives of 3W and 173.

For sure, we had experienced many ups and downs to this point, but the up side was predominant. The common thread was the simple act of praying together! In our life together it had become so natural, so easy and relaxing. It was what we always looked forward to after being apart! When starting this outline, it had never actually occurred to me that here was the strength that had led us both to accomplish so many tasks. This power also kept us hopeful for the future. Could I in some way influence or help others to find that wonderful secret to a rewarding life?

The Two Of Us, 1969

Now you know why the family autobiography turned into a published book. While it is my hope that the life story holds some interest to the reader, it is intended to reveal how the simple, joyful, and crucial act of regular prayer as a couple can make life so worthwhile!

It does not guarantee that you're going to be prosperous, with lavish lifestyle and possessions. Nor does it mean you will have perfect health or never experience downturns or severe disappointments. However, it does mean satisfaction, strength beyond belief, forgiveness, and peace of mind. God always seemed to be nearby and when we were at a point of deciding which was the best way to go, the answer was there even when we least expected it!

How in the world did Eli ever put up with me! I was gone so much: Meetings, trips, nights at the office, afternoons on the golf course, president of this and that, when was I ever at home? She was so patient, supportive and loving! Still, we were so close and seemed to always find ways to be excited over big and little things. There was no doubt she was just as active in her world as I was in mine. We rejoiced in each other's successes and accomplishments. How we remained so "calm" is still a wonder but yet I come back to those simple words: "Pray together."

CHAPTER 25

"Christmas:" A time to Witness for Christ!

1969

A sales record was set this year of 1969: $59.7 million. If only ½ million better than 1968, we had regained our position in the market place. To improve shipments of our aluminum fishing boats several large railroad cars were purchased, displaying the Mirro name coast to coast. More changes had also taken place. The over-taxed computer was upgraded with two IBM 360 units. (An interesting note: the Lap Top unit I'm typing this on probably has more capacity than those two million dollar monsters!) Color Porcelain coating of cookware, as developed by the engineers, was centralized in Plant #5. All products to be so coated was shipped to this location. This was the beginning of an overall "automation" changes to be implemented some ten years later.

It became clear we were not grooming younger personnel to someday take over important plant management positions. Another observation; there were too many levels of command in management between me and the worker (Namely: Supervisor, Foreman, General Foreman, Superintendent, Plant Manager and Gen.Plt .Manager). Added to this, most had an assistant, making up to at least eleven levels between me and that important worker! Tradition had developed this long chain-of-command and in no way could it change overnight. They were all good, hardworking and long-term employees, and many were nearing possible retirement.

A new program was developed called "Up-Date" training for the manufacturing division. Present factory management and other persons with potential of advancement were selected and placed in this training program. In a one on one manner, each was shown and explained the purpose of each department. They spent time in all aspects of labor, from office to sales to finance--- records, controls, operations, and shipping! When finished, they had witnessed every function of the total business and all of the many plants. It was recognized as a privilege to be chosen for this training that took weeks to complete. We hired some new young college engineers and placed them through the same training. It proved to produce some fine future management people. Each participant was rated by the different department heads visited and this was used to determine best candidates for promotion.

Becoming an officer of the company also had some very rewarding tasks as well. A top event was to recognize employees of the manufacturing group achieving 25years or more with Mirro! A special dinner banquet was planned each year which would include families. It was my honor to greet each one, thanking them for their service. Another honor: Each year the Mirro Management Club held a Christmas dinner party (which included families). This first year as an officer, I was approached and asked if I would give the Christmas after-dinner speech. While not a tradition, this was an important opportunity, and, like others, I asked what subject I should select as a relative newcomer. I was told that I could speak on anything, even the Christmas Story! That night at home, Eli was asked her opinion. "It's a Christmas Party; why not the Christmas Story!" So that is what I did, built around a contemporary happening. My only regret is that I cannot recall specifically what I said! But this I do remember; every Christmas thereafter, they requested that I "give the Christmas message" at the family banquet. May I quote a note received from a person attending the dinner?

"CHRISTMAS:" A TIME TO WITNESS FOR CHRIST!

"My wife and I thought you gave a very appropriate talk the other night at----. We enjoyed listening. I hope you continue with this type of talk at future gatherings. It is very heartwarming to know that we have such dedication to Jesus Christ in our midst, especially someone in a position such as yours. It becomes contagious. I'm sure He will help keep our company strong if we continue with such dedication to Him. Thank you. Sincerely, XXXXX"

What a real honor. I am only thankful and humbled!

Being on the board of directors was a very enlightening and educational experience. I won't attempt to explain or go into detail as to its function or makeup. Rather, I will try to relate some of my personal reactions and participation. Meetings were held quarterly. Each year at least one meeting was held at Manitowoc or another city where an operating plant was located. It was always my pleasure to give the members a tour of one these facilities. From the first meeting, all members seemed very interested in asking me questions regarding the operations---why and how this or that was accomplished. What I saw in the future and what my plans might be. It soon became obvious why I was asked to be on the Board. Again, this was a strong reason for me to do my homework, planning for the future! Put that aside for a moment. Though big business in our day is not always perceived as operating very ethically, the Mirro board of directors was exemplary. Mr. A Vits (Chairman) and Mr. C. W. Ziemer (President) were men of high integrity and of impeccable morals; while I may not always have agreed with their business decisions, I admired them immensely. Their predecessors must have been made from the same cloth. Each membership of the Board fit this pattern. Pete Bolliger (Partner Foley & Lardner), Norman Ott (Mkt. Consultant, a major stockholder), Sam Simmons (VP, Alcoa), Dr. Bob Spitzer (President, Murphy Products) all in my estimation were wonderful, honest and hardworking men. After meeting with them and hearing their input as well as witnessing them in action, I soon could judge them as individuals of substance. All were inspirations to me and so willing to accept me as a partner in reaching important

IS GOD ON OUR SIDE?

decisions for the Mirro Company. Board members who take their fiduciary responsibilities seriously are a very important part of our free enterprise system in this country.

While speaking of my admiration for "honest, hardworking people of togetherness" what about the wonderful family at home!

> *February 11, 1969.*
>
> *Our new dining room table arrived -- feel like I'm in some mansion-- can't reach across the table, every meal seems a banquet. Very lovely. Miss the old chrome set -- it weathered with us -- part of home, felt comfortable with it.*
>
> *Nancy has been digging in with sewing -- decided to make several outfits at last minute. Early planning makes for enjoyable sewing, so she has finished a pair of cotton culottes and almost ready for hem on a red print cotton shirt, has tucked front with piping along the edges. She is so patient now and works very well -- she knows when she's had it and quickly sets aside for another day.*
>
> *Talk about proud -- can burst our buttons over Louise. 1st semester grades arrived -- -- get this!*
>
> *Physics - A., calculus - A., history - B., English - B plus, religion - A.*
>
> *That makes a 3.625 average, out of a possible 4.0 -- wow! What discipline and hard work into her freshman year, she loves it, this is her joy -- Luther and studying -- so great to be with someone so happy in what they are doing -- so happy with friends -- blessing to have them come to this point.*
>
> *Nancy so happy too -- just wants and wishes she could stay*

"CHRISTMAS:" A TIME TO WITNESS FOR CHRIST!

16, and right where she is -- everything is as she would like it. Tom just content -- works hard -- we are much blessed!

Our big news! February 4, 1969, Richard N. Thomsen, elected to the board of directors of the Mirro Aluminum Company. Yes, it's true -- we can't believe it -- all this recognition should be given to Dick for his work -- as the song goes and what Tom plays on the organ "The Impossible Dream"-- -- -- Dick dared to dream that impossible dream -- our theme song for 1969. He found out about this promotion at the directors' meeting in Chicago, where he was invited to give a report on the manufacturing status of the company. His appointment was in our paper -- over the radio all day -- in the Milwaukee Journal -- in the Wall Street Journal -- all too tremendous!

March 16 & 17, 1969.

Today, our Nancy treated us by serving the Lord with her talents -- she played a piano solo for the offertory at those services. The organist gave her background. She played Waltz in A flat by Brahms -- so proud of her performance. On Valentine's Day -- florist range. The doorbell -- Louise sent a beautiful long stemmed red rose with love to her family!

Another honor for Dick last Thursday. He went to the monthly meeting of the Society for Advancement of Management. After dinner, they surprised him with the recognition of his achievements in the past years, most recently VP and Board of Directors. We don't clamor for honor, but when it received is a great thing to know others recognize what you have done, so thrilled for Dick.

IS GOD ON OUR SIDE?

September 24, 1969.

This weekend, the band is traveling to Madison to join other high school bands at halftime, Wisconsin football game. Dick will drive one of the busloads. Tom and Nancy are thrilled with their new band instructor at high school. Tom has quit work at the drugstore, last Saturday, started work at the library. Can now earn $1.16 per hour -- can get average of 16 hours per week. Not too demanding -- gives him ample time for lessons and music.

December 3, 1969.

----Most thrilling to tell -- (Tom) last Sunday, gave the sermon at church, both services, for annual youth Sunday. He does like public speaking, and he did a fine job. He chose his own topic -- worked up his own presentation, no one corrected it, believe me, till I read it -- held my breath -- it was going over the radio to the whole community! He was challenging all to let the childhood images of God die -- mature -- through study, then the witness. He used Scripture passages such as "When I was a child I spoke like a child"; "Let the redeemed of the Lord say so!". The world presents many gods -- do we accept the true God in Jesus Christ.

And now our big news! We are going to spend Christmas with the Thomsen's (Grandparents) in Phoenix! 11 years since our last trip there -- can hardly believe it is possible. We leave on the 22nd and come back on January 6. You better believe we are jumping with joy. Dick mentioned to salesmen from Kaiser Aluminum that we were flying out and taking the family. The gentleman presented Dick with 5 tickets to the Rose Bowl game in California! What a wonderful opportunity and experience for all 5 of us. Dick is working double

"CHRISTMAS:" A TIME TO WITNESS FOR CHRIST!

time for the 2 ½ weeks that he'll be taking off, so glad he will finally take a vacation and that we can spend Christmas with the Thomsens.

Both Tom and Nancy made the honor roll on their last report card -- so proud of them. Tom, being active in dramatics and tennis clubs. Nancy again won competition to be in the honorary swim club, and busily working up routines for the May aqua ballet. Saturday, Nancy takes her college tests -- this the only requirement left for her application to Luther. She was initiated into National Honorary Math Club, took a lot of years, she finally got with it in school and loves it -- literally does -- can't dig in hard enough; she was moved to advanced Math and Physics class as she was doing so well!

Brass quartet going along with couples club when we go caroling tomorrow night, Tom has lead Coronet! Saturday and Sunday afternoon, he will play at the mall shopping center, organ, then for Christmas program Sunday night he will be in the brass quartet again. This weekend filled with music.

Can you guess what our dog likes for breakfast? Rice Krispy's! Can listen to them snap, crackle and pop before she eats them -- really a nut! Sits there with the happiest look, as they snap away. After that, outside in the snow is her delight. She sticks her nose in the snow and runs along like a snow plow. Rolls and kicks up the flakes and just smiles with happiness.

Lesson #9

Let us all "Witness for Christ"

CHAPTER 26

"Eli the True Witness"
in our Family and to others

1970

1970 began another full, new year of adventure! Ha, youth! At the ripe old age of 45, for me there was no stopping to take a deep breath. The planning process had become extremely exciting for me. Establishing that 40-year look into the future proved to be more of a challenge than I first thought. Charts were plotted for the 40 prior years (1930-1970) sales versus employment, plant space, capital expenditures and area population. To make this meaningful, inflation had to be factored in and notations of important happenings inserted. Ratios of each factor were also established. With trend lines extended for the next 40 years, I could predict the future if no changes were to take place such as indicated by the important happenings. When all was said and done, it was so obvious that the projections were impossible and that there would never be enough man power (or other factors) to meet the sales growth projected matching past figures! Some very big important happenings had to take place! A challenge was given to the engineers to come up with some ideas. How could we reduce the requirements projected for space and labor as we increased our volume?

Now that the combined computer forecasting, Production Planning and Control system was operating, the Corporate Operations Review Board was established. It consisted of VP of Sales, I and the Secretary Treasurer. On a regular basis we examined variances from standard and plan; changing direction if warranted, trying to improve or fine tune areas that seemed inconsistent with our long range objectives. It proved to be very effective and gave each one of us a better insight into the total operation. It improved and supported teamwork. Each could relate the findings to our individual staffs and set required objectives or changes in motion. Improved customer service, plus substantial reduction in inventory, was an early achievement.

This group then proposed the "PAR" (Planning, Action and Results) program. Every manager would establish a Specific Measurable Plan (Objective) for the coming year. This would be approved by the Review Board as to its viability and monetary value. If it was successfully accomplished by year's end the person would receive an established dollar bonus. The cost of the program became a part of the department's budget. It not only encouraged each department to be self-supporting, but it was also an incentive to each person to increase their income. At the same time this program was established, it now became each manager's responsibility to submit their budget for their responsibilities in the coming year.

Another innovation was added to the computer system. Every product was rated as to its importance to customers. For example, there were basic items that nearly every customer placed on order in every shipment. These would receive a priority letter of "A". These items by nature became the high volume items to be produced and it was important to always have in stock for immediate shipment. Thus was developed a ranking of all products in regard to their importance in sales and in production schedules and finished goods inventory. This also provided margin classifications to sales for concentration of most profitable items to sell. But more important to me, it indicated what items needed cost reduction studies to improve profit margins. All items were classified and identified therefore by volume, profit and importance to determine inventory and scheduling sequence.

On-time shipping and customer satisfaction showed much improvement almost immediately.

With all this going on at the office a few other happenings kept me active outside those brick walls. My counterparts in local industry politely recommended my becoming active in different societies. I was selected to be on the "Governor's New Product of the year Awards" committee. I was one of five Professional Engineers in the state of Wisconsin to work with Governor Warren Knowles---quite an honor and a new experience. Being active in labor negotiation, it was important to work with other individuals in the state with similar responsibilities. This group was part of the Northeast Wisconsin Industrial Association which included members from some 60 firms and banks. This year they chose to elect me a director of the association, and in 1971, I became VP. The Gillett, Wisconsin plant was now in operation and monthly visits were on my calendar. With it came the requests to speak to and visit local clubs and groups, both civic and industrial. The Manitowoc workers' union requested representation at this new plant. The employees chose not to be represented by the union. The year, 1970, was the 75th anniversary for Mirro. I was privileged to attend many of the celebrations held throughout the season.

The National Cookware Association, made up of nearly all manufactures of like items, held an annual meeting at any one of many resort areas. It was my pleasure to be invited on many of these enlightening trips where it was possible to meet and discuss mutual problems with competitors. Wives were invited and it was a chance for the better half to mingle with their counterparts. Examples of area visited: Biltmore Country Club, Phoenix, Arizona, Grand Hotel, Bermuda, Lake Lawn Lodge, Wisconsin, Green Brier, Virginia, and the Doral Resort, South Florida. Naturally, following informative meetings each day, golf was a daytime pleaser and very special meals were enjoyed. This was far from what Eli and Dick Thomsen were accustomed to and something we really never felt comfortable participating in, however we certainly enjoyed the opportunity.

◂ IS GOD ON OUR SIDE?

Eli was rapidly included in every activity for the wives and her ever-present smile always attracted a group. What a plus for me and how proud I was of her! One trip to Bermuda we ventured out on rented Mopeds. Since Bermuda was a British Colony, we had to concentrate on driving on the left side of the road. We had a blast and got to see the total island. Best of all, being invited every other or so year, it was a chance for the two of us to forget the chores of home and get to know and enjoy each other---an opportunity to recharge the batteries.

Mirro entered the boat business early in the 1960s and rapidly gained an excellent reputation in the fishing boat category. Boats consumed many pounds of aluminum sheeting that we could produce in our Rolling Mill. The mill is most profitable and efficient when operated on a 3-shift basis. The boat production was a big contributor in improving the company's bottom line. One negative to the boat field, however, was the marketing/sales area---a rather foreign animal in the cookware world. In 1971, Mirro announced the purchase of Cruisers Inc. of Oconto, Wisconsin, quality manufacturer of fiberglass pleasure boats. They had the outlets, dealers and know-how of the industry. It could improve the sales of our fishing craft, plus expand the product line. Mr. Roy Thompson, President of Cruisers, also became a board member and, in short order, a very close friend of mine. He was often reminded of the wrong spelling of his name but I forgave him for that because his birth date was June 26th, the same as mine.

Yes, God was on my side this year, but I now wonder why? I was the same person I had been all through the years! Sure, I had more experience under my belt and a bit more confidence in making decisions, but still I was just a young engineer trying to keep his head above water. I can only attribute much of the success to my family, who were not only supportive but led by my Christian wife and wonderful mother! What a tremendous witness and example to the children and to *me*. Our nightly prayers (whenever home) were a key to ever remind me what was most important in our lives! Have you sensed that feeling as you have read her letters? Oh how I miss those hours with her! A few more examples follow. She was so involved with the children; note the letter of Sept 3rd in particular, expressing something as simple as her feelings regarding God's creation in the sky! (And again in the ending words of the Nov. 18th & Dec 11th letters.)

January 19, 1970.

Our trip to Phoenix was terrific. Dad and mom had spent much time getting ready for us. We stayed with the folks a full week. Then we rented a car and drove to California, first to San Diego, then up the coast to LA. Saw the beautiful Rose Bowl Parade then the Rose Bowl game. Friday the 2nd, found us at Disneyland till 10:30 PM. Another unforgettably day. Had a chance to visit with one of Dick's roommates from University. (Working on the Space Shuttle) Then traveled to San Bernardino, winding up in Palm Springs. We boarded a Swiss tramway car to the high peaks, a cable ride that has to be the bone chilling ride of a lifetime. We soon were back in Phoenix with mom and dad for a warm dinner waiting for us.

They Do Grow Up! 1970; Nancy, Tom, Louise

◀ IS GOD ON OUR SIDE?

Mom and Dad Grow Up Too!

April 8, 1970.

Nancy is our creative member in the family. Working many long hours, producing a delicate stuffed Civil War doll, about 17 inches high. Made for a close friend from last summer. She has done an outstanding job, the period clothing, adding details and fashioning a wig to fit. She is so proud -- hates to give it up -- real giving of love.

So very proud of Tom, on good Friday at church -- had an excellent message and delivered it well. He dictates to me -- helps the process to move on quickly. Add to that the high school band concert before Easter was just great. Tom's trumpet solo came off very well. Can't miss that tall, handsome guy in the brass section. Next weekend -- the 17th -- is the high school prom, and Tom is all butterflies, anticipating the day.

Dick was in Milwaukee last Saturday attending a management seminar and giving a speech. Also busy last week, giving a Bethel Bible lesson at church. Earlier Dick and I were invited to the Gillette, Wisconsin community meeting where the Mirro executives were invited for their Chamber of Commerce dinner. It was to honor the company for bringing the new industry into their town. Along with all of these happenings, I was to be a congregational delegate to the District convention of the ELC in Green Bay.

June 24, 1970

Church summer Bible school ran from June 8-19, my preparation for it heaviest in April and May. Much discussion for classroom time -- -- excellent reference material and visual aids for teaching. All the teachers excited about the challenge. We had 166 students! 62 teachers, assistants and helpers. Most re-warding service for me! So happy I can do it for the church and the students. The enthusiasm of the students, the opportunity given to them, the rewards to the teachers -- -- no problem too difficult to surmount knowing so much was accomplished.

All 3 kids made us most proud with their schoolwork. This last year all finished on the honor roll. It was graduation year for Nancy! It was a beautiful day for her; graduation exercises held outside: we laughed as she said she was worried and concerned about Tom. He was chosen to play taps at the end of the ceremony, climbing to the high tower at the school to perform-- -- Tom detests heights-- --but all went well. Nancy looked just radiant! Pleased as punch, and her joy just radiated!

Tom is working evenings with the Drama Company, this year working on "Guys and Dolls" He is in charge of props and transportation. Has a "walk on" part and also in the chorus line. At church he was elected president of our Luther league.

IS GOD ON OUR SIDE?

September 3, 1970.

Last week of August, Tom was hired at the local drugstore, a great opportunity to earn a little extra money

Before school started, we took a family vacation, the cottage at Stormy Lake, Wisconsin, from August 17 -- 21. The weather was great. The cottage is facing to the north, the moon eclipse with the Northern lights in complete fullness was the highlight of our stay -- -- <u>all heaven proclaimed God's power and majesty -- all that was missing were the Angels heralding. We took the boat to the middle of the lake at 9:45 PM watching all the wonders of the sky.</u> We all had a great time together, the week went by too rapidly, we soon were back to reality in Manitowoc.

With the aid of a borrowed station wagon, and with the family Buick packed to its fullest, the 2 girls were off to college, even with a bicycle. Once on campus, and with 5 of us put to work, all was quickly unloaded and brought to the 2 girls rooms.

October 20, 1970.

Layman's Sunday at our church was on October 11. Dick was one of 4 men to give the sermon, speaking on spiritual security -- his joy in being a Christian. What a terrific witness -- our buttons burst! From a pastor, you would expect it -- from a layman -- "all of the sudden you want to get up and be counted too" -- that's the comment we received from many that day. Joyous day, sharing with him.

Dick has been elected to board of directors of the North East Wisconsin industrial Association. The association is made of many of the industrial firms in this part of Wisconsin. Working together to improve industry in this part of the state. Dick's father had belonged to a similar group when he worked in Fort Atkinson -- Kenosha -- so we knew that he would be proud that his son followed in his footsteps. He gave many speeches to the various district organizations.

November 18, 1970.

Dick volunteered to take a group of young people from our church to visit the different Lutheran colleges in our area. Before the trip was over they had traveled more than 1000 miles. Tom had already applied for admission to Luther College in Decorah, Iowa but he so enjoyed seeing the colleges! His course intentions were English and "Pre-sem"-- only time and the Lord's guidance will tell what He has planned for Tom.

December 11, 1970.

Royal treatment received last weekend on a trip to Pittsburgh, Pennsylvania, had difficulty believing it was me! Private jet landed at our airport, 7:30 AM Sunday morning. We were guests of Alcoa for the weekend. 2 limousines awaited us at the Pittsburgh airport, zoomed us into mid-Pittsburgh to the 3 Rivers Stadium. Lunch served in the special observation box to watch the Packers play the Pittsburg Steelers. Radiant heaters in the ceiling of the box, what real comfort and the Green Bay Packers won! After the game, the limousines whisked us to the hotel. Private dining room -- Pvt. Cook and waiters -- waiters, one for every 2 people! Too much! What a different world! Obvious I was not accustomed to this -- I watch the waiters more than he tended us! Monday morning the men had breakfast at 7:30 -- off to business for the day, while the women went shopping and toured the high spots of Pittsburgh. Never believed so many fantastic things to happen to me in such a short time. Following day, we were back on the plane, which was fitted out with lounge chairs -- what a lush comfort. Perhaps I've lingered too long, telling you about this entire trip, but I guess it's so unbelievable! I have to keep telling myself it happened, please forgive my chatter.

Tom used slides in a sermon that he presented at church -- -- any number of phone calls, if any indication, the sermon was well received and accepted. His title "What a great thing it is". He brought in, what a great thing to have the right kind of peace -- Christ's peace in your heart -- through home, church, Christian Fellowship. <u>*When he practiced his sermons for me earlier -- many gulps and tears to hold back, how he had found that much joy in life and true meaning of being a Christian. Joy and thanksgiving for his faith. Parents can only pray that their children will hold onto that faith and let it continually guide their living.*</u>

I have been busy planning the Sunday school Christmas program for the 5-6th graders -- -- also the women's Christmas program entitled "Let the prophets speak" -- very inspirational -- -- then the Circle Christmas Bible study, where one of my friends works with me.

CHAPTER 27

Mirro Corp. Stock Available!
Fed Price Controls!

1971-'73

With only one-year labor contracts signed with the Machinist Union, I had the feeling that we were in negotiations year round. However, relations seemed to improve each year. This year (1971) we agreed to a 21-month contract. While today it may seem rather mundane, as the computer era was in its infancy, the telephone business was still the most vital means of communication. The company entered into contract with AT&T for use of the Watts line.

A flat monthly fee allowed for unlimited long distance calls. Spending many night hours at the office, it was possible for me (and often, family members) to make calls to our parents. It was so helpful and we were very grateful for this.

The year, 1972, saw Mirro reach a new level of sales volume: $80.4 million! This was a 17% increase over the previous year and a 20% increase in earnings! Much could be attributed to our new "computer control programs" that precipitated improved customer service and controlled reduced inventory. As mentioned, Mr. Sam Simmons of Alcoa was a member of our board. An Alcoa officer had been in this position for many years. When aluminum was first developed in mass production, it was considered a rather precious metal. I have heard that eating utensils made of this shining lightweight material were given to the royalty of England as a special gift! Alcoa was looking for manufacturers to develop product-consuming volumes of this new metal. The founders of a small company in Wisconsin that grew to be the Mirro of today received financial backing in this development. From that point on, a representative of Alcoa was present on our board of directors to help and to oversee their interest. They represented approximately 20% ownership of the company. This was fine until now. But we had grown to be the largest producer of cookware in the world. At the same time, a division of Alcoa called "Wear Ever" had also grown to be a large producer of aluminum cookware. The Federal Government now claimed a conflict of interest on the part of Alcoa and required them to divest of one or the other. At that point, 211,770 shares of Mirro common stock was to be sold on the NY Stock exchange. What a learning experience for this young engineer as I was growing in knowledge of the business world. If someone were to purchase this total block of stock being released by Alcoa, unwanted or disruptive changes could be forced on Mirro's management. Mr. Simmons made sure this did not happen. The shares owned by Alcoa were dispersed through a number of brokers throughout the country who, in turn, distributed it to many individual clients.

Before becoming a member of the Mirro Board of Directors, the role of this group was only a far off and vague conception. It didn't take long for me to realize their importance. Make up seems to vary company to company. In our company it was made up of eight people, four employed (all officers including the CEO) and four prominent business persons. Only the outside directors were assigned specific duties including auditing and executive compensation. We were all submitted to stockholder approval via annual stock holder meetings. The outside members held the responsibility for selecting President-CEO. Officers from each function (marketing/sales, Finance/treasurer and manufacturing) from within were there to present the plans, actions and progress of their specific areas of responsibility. Before my first meeting as a member, Mr. Fred Terens and Mr. L.

MIRRO CORP. STOCK AVAILABLE! FED PRICE CONTROLS!

Newberry helped me by giving me minutes of past meetings, which gave me an idea of what was expected in a report. Meetings were held quarterly, usually at Pittsburgh, Milwaukee, or Manitowoc--- these being the cities where directors were located.

At the home office, the Federal Government was also giving me lots to plan for and to assign responsibility. A new requirement called OSHA (Occupational Safety) was posted by Congress. Fortunately we anticipated its enactment so compliance was not too difficult. However, the paper work proved to be the usual mountain of tree-cutting paper work specified by dear Uncle Sam. This is an example of Fed Regulations that was required for reporting at each director's meeting. Not only was there much to learn and in a rather short period of time but a much self- imposed demand in the area of planning for the changes I hoped for in the future.

In 1973, more regulations caused dire results to the operations of companies and businesses in this country. The government imposed price controls! Material shortages in many parts of the country were starting to push prices upward. As material and labor costs increased and we could not increase our selling prices, profit margins began to shrink. Sales were up nearly 8.5% but profits reduced. There was some good news, however. It was evident that relations with our employees were improving. We signed three labor contracts with the labor unions, the two major contracts with the production workers and the crafts (machinist and electricians) contract was for three years! I feel the workers were happy and so was I. With the continual growth in sales, plans were laid for increased 2nd and 3rd shift operations in nearly all plants. In the published annual report for the year I was privileged to answer several important questions to stock holders;

    Q. "Are material shortages affecting Mirro?"

    A. "There was no noticeable effect in 1973. We were able to obtain all necessary materials and the same situation is holding true up to present in 1974. The lead time required from suppliers did increase dramatically in the last half of 1973 and currently makes it necessary to anticipate requirements much sooner than what was considered normal in the past. We are confident that, with the aid of our latest computer scheduling system, we can meet the future supply challenge successfully."

Q. "Is there a shortage of aluminum?"

A. "The world demand for aluminum exceeds the available supply and this condition may exist for the next several years. In our case, with the basic versatility of aluminum and its application to our product lines, present indications from suppliers in the first quarter indicate adequate supplies. In addition, our long record as a substantial purchaser will give us a fair share. We have always purchased on the domestic market and kept excellent customer relations with our prime suppliers. Our ability to recycle aluminum in our own rolling mill would also be particularly advantageous in the possible event of a future shortage."

Q. "What effect will the energy shortage directly have on your manufacturing operations?"

A. "While there appears to be a real energy shortage, our utility suppliers indicate assurance of furnishing adequate energy to Mirro in 1974. A corporate energy committee has been established within the company to ensure that we live up to our responsibility and needs."

Q. "What is Mirro's labor supply situation?"

A. We saw a substantial increase in our labor force in 1973. Most of this was utilized in the expansion of our second and third shift operations of present facilities. Our relations with the labor unions continue to be excellent and we believe this trend should continue."

The cost of aluminum ingot was beginning to reach unheard of new highs! In this year of '73, ingot costs increased from 21 cents in January to 29 cents per pound in December. That was approximately a 40% increase in the most consumer-purchased segment when manufacturing cook ware! Fortunately, later in the year, the feds allowed relief and price increases of produced products. As I write this in the year 2008-9, I can't help but compare that which happened in'73 to the present. One of most notable shortages then was gasoline. Not only was the cost of product going up but that of transporting---another factor under my responsibility. Yes, costs of most every item available was increasing, wages were on the increase, and inflation was on the rise. Could we be headed in the same direction today as we see more and more government regulation entering our lives in the U.S.?

In 1974, aluminum ingot reached another new high of 39 cents per pound. Over a period close to one year, this represented an increase of 85%. I had many meetings with Bob Franz, purchasing manager, and we established close communications with all of our aluminum suppliers such as Alcoa, Reynolds, Kaiser and Alcan. We were able to level out these large and rapid changes by entering into longer term contracts, stipulating a price that would hold constant for a foreseeable future date, then, at that time, renegotiating a new contract. This proved to be an excellent approach which also committed us to the purchase of a fixed quantity over the stated time period. This again was made possible through our ability to project usage following the sales forecast into the future. You might say "Forecasts are never right so how can you possibly rely on them to commit such a large dollar outlay?" With the use of the new IBM computers, sales forecasts were revised continually, with immediate printouts reflecting material requirements. The error factor, while still there, was reduced substantially. Again I was so fortunate to have a knowledgeable and experienced staff with which to work. Many a trip to suppliers was made to see their plants and, most important, gain the confidence and respect of the supplier's staff, letting them know our needs and problems and we, in turn, hearing and seeing theirs.

This was a rather pivotal year for me at Mirro. I loved my work and enjoyed the people I worked with. Mr. Ziemer (President) was a fine Christian man and you could always feel comfortable when with him, whether at work, traveling, or in off duty activities. I did not always agree with his business decisions or approach and I told him so, but he was considerate and honest in all he did. Frank Prescott (Vice President Mkt/Sales) was another fine gentleman that became a sounding board for me. His history, experience, and knowledge of the industry were outstanding and his willingness to keep me in his confidence was much appreciated. He taught me the ropes and ways of Mirro. Urial Garey (Secretary Treasurer) whom I also played golf with regularly at Branch Country Club was very helpful. We had excellent relations these first nine years. But his cigars about drove me nuts, especially when I was required to ride with him any distance in an auto.

For the past several years the engineering group was expending major effort on the "A" products. An example was the "Pressure Cookers". How could we reduce the costs, maintain or improve quality and reduce the time to manufacture. This, in turn, could reduce lead times required to order materials which automatically reduced inventory costs. All capital expenditures were to be recovered through these designed cost reductions within five years of operation. This was agreed on by the finance people to be a good return on investment. Capital expenditures for 1974 were $2.4 million. Over 80% of this was for machinery purchased to increase productivity and the cost reduction programs. Included were eight large mechanical drawing presses, several of these for the "Pressure Cookers" mentioned above. Twelve additional new presses were scheduled for installation in 1975 or early 1976.

It was early in 1973 that we began planning for this improvement in the production of the pressure cooker line of product. The marketing department then planned a large scale promotion of the product line for the year 1975 with country wide advertising. With the poor economic picture, canning and home cooking was on the rise. While our engineers were very capable of major programs of this nature, our lap of work in front of us was just overflowing; overtime was readily spent. The need for more tool and die design, plus machine shop work, was exceeding our capacity.

In my past years of experience, the use of consultants and outside talent was often found very worthwhile. When I was part owner of the Heiden Company, one of the three partners was Tom Hauge. The two of us had equal respect for each other's talents, but I really felt second rate to Tom when it came to automatic machine design systems. Tom had been a tool and die engineer at Mirro early in his career, later to join Heiden just as I had. He, too, left Heidens to start his own small Company in Manitowoc, engineering automation equipment and production lines. He was successful in submitting a quotation with an excellent designed production line for the "Pressure Cookers". When in operation in 1975, it proved to beat the savings projected with a payback of less than five years.

As I said earlier, these were pivotal years for me. All in the manufacturing division were now confident we were on the right track and also were being recognized as capable of improving margins, producing more with less and little or no need for increased floor space. When attending seminars, both in New York and among Professional Engineer locally, the concept of CPM was introduced. (CPM: Critical Path Method) This was very simple when applied properly---a wonderful tool to predict time to complete and how to reduce time to complete a given project. A given project had to be broken down into individual tasks, time required for each of these tasks, what tasks could be done simultaneously, or which overlapped. It involved graphically laying out in sequence the total of all tasks and applying dates from start to finish. Sounds simple but it does take knowledge of each task and the time to consult those involved in each. Once all is laid out, it will point out just where the main Critical Path begins and ends. To reduce the total time of the project, you need only to concentrate on that one line of tasks that is critical. It was to become so important in the future that it required the full time of one engineer.

Now there were three college students to keep track of at home! A bit of a strain on the budget, although each was diligent in their use of monies, and even found work to cover some expenses---all at Luther College! (Fortunately, the banks also saw fit to permit a loan!) The house seemed so empty. But mother stayed very active at church and letters were frequent both ways. Then our first born hit us with a big and wonderful surprise! There were also some memorable perks to let us relax together! These letters will explain!

May 15, 1971.

I could write a book -- -- what a vacation! Dick and I flew to Phoenix, Arizona, where Dick attended a Metal Cookware Association; we stayed in a cabana attached to the Frank Lloyd Wright Hotel. A thrill flying in and out of Manitowoc, and seeing our city from the air -- -- great flight from Chicago on a 747. Word drifted out that it was my birthday -- and for the final banquet on the 7th, the whole group toasted me with champagne -- how about that! Sunday while Dick was in meetings, <u>I walked to a mountain top , alone, singing hymns</u> -- --just me, the lizards and the bees!

While in Phoenix. We visited Mom and Pappy; they introduced us to friends (retired president of Abbott laboratories), who was a model railroad enthusiast and noted for his great modeling work throughout the United States. What a wonderful experience for Dick.

November 21, 1971.

For me, our "snip and sew" group at church, turned out 180 quilts. This past year! All made from scraps, remnants, old drapes plus, nimble fingers, and good fellowship, bringing love to others. While Dick is much involved at work, our new pastor wonders if I'm married. Never sees me with my husband. Our older pastor comments, "She'd better be, there are 3 Thomsen students at Luther College!" then the younger pastor looked at me and wondered how come I didn't have a job. My answer, "Well, fortunately, <u>I can spend my time serving the Lord</u> and letting Dick earn our living! Sure great for me!"

One of the local doctors and friends have been biking early in the mornings, -- -- invited Dick to join them. 6:30 AM he is out biking, pedals until 7:15, back for shower and then off to work by 7:45.

November 29, 1971.

First of all, you must know Louise's big news -- -- she is engaged! So all right, I feel old, already! Just as the age I was when there were stars in my eyes. Yes, still have them -- but oh, young love! She is off floating. The young man -- Lon Horton -- is a physics major at Luther.

December 29, 1971.

Our church services were such an up lift -- <u>a renewal of joy in Christ</u> -- -- A Christian Fellowship. That will uphold us for many days. We are fortunate to have many active and talented laymen to help our pastors -- together all have given *so much as they shared Christ in their lives.*

Louise is quitting work on the 31st -- that will give her one week of wedding planning. Next week will be busy shopping -- planning -- looking. Looks most favorable for being in June!

December 13, 1972.

Tom has a full schedule, working as a guard at the Mirro plants. Nancy, of course, has all kinds of baking plans. Come January 1, Tom will go to Milwaukee for 4 weeks with a Lutheran church, working with the Pastors and the Next Door Coffeehouse.

Nancy is definitely accepted at Wilton School of cake decorating and candy making located in Chicago -- -- her interim elective for 2 weeks. January 8 -- 19th.

March 30th, Dick was awarded the Silver Knight Award by the American Management Association at a dinner meeting. I knew of it in advance, but a surprise to Dick. He gave a most challenging acceptance speech; outdid the luncheon speaker.

May 5, 1973

The spring Metal Cookware Association meeting was held in Bermuda! It is truly fabulous, God's creation at its prime with people who love and are proud of their island. I walked almost 8 miles a day observing native birds, plants, trees -- -- a thrill to see fields of Easter lilies in bloom.

<u>*Christ's peace, to each of you -- -- may each new day dawning be a joy in His presence for you.*</u>

July 5, 1973

Busy schedules here. Nancy gets up at 4 AM, Dick up with her and peddles along to the bakery. Tom works at Mirro as a guard -- -- his hours are 3:30 -- 11:30 PM, also as a 2nd job 3 days a week, hours 8 AM to 2:30 PM.

July 2, 1973.

Nancy continues to get many cake orders, reputation is getting around. Alsothe bakery is very pleased with her work and giving her more orders to fill -- -- longer hours.

Dick started a new hobby -- tailoring. Made a light yellow sports jacket, and print slacks.

July 24, 1973

If you can't lick them -- join them! Family talk about a bike trip in August -- -- no duffers allowed -- so who gets up at sunrise to bike ride, but yours truly! Now I ride with Nancy like dad does, total round-trip of 6 miles.

August 26, we will pick up Louise and Lon, then bike the Elroy-Sparta Bike Trail (38 miles each way).this is the old railroad track with rails removed and made for biking.

IS GOD ON OUR SIDE?

September 29 1973.

1ˢᵗ letter received today from Tom! Nottingham, England -- -- churches -- stone hedge -- much to see, people extremely friendly, purchased a bicycle, but finds dangerous to ride.

CHAPTER 28

Changes in Marketing/Sales; Automation the Word In Manufacturing

1974 to 1979

In the years of 1974-75, employment exceeded the 3,000 level, as located in 12 different plants of operation. Due to our loyal, hard-working employees, we had become known as the world's largest manufacturer of stamped aluminum cookware. Products included cooking and baking utensils, small electrical appliances, pressure cookers and canners, house siding, camping cookware, aluminum boats, toys and foil containers. Added to this was the manufacture of fiberglass pleasure boats and supplier to other manufactures with contracted stampings and components for their products. (Examples of contract items: Auto parts for Chrysler, GM, and Ford; parts for dish and clothes washers, name brand products for GE, Sunbeam, Doremeyer, Westinghouse, Maytag, Country Fried Chicken Corp, Holiday Inns.) The cookware-appliance category accounted for 90% of our total volume. In 1975 a new milestone was reached; sales achieved $100,281,122.00. When I joined the company just ten years earlier, sales were $59 million; I had been privileged to be part of this fine group, and to see its sales nearly double; what a good feeling to be a part of this exciting growth!

I can't say enough about the fine and loyal employees and their families. Sons and daughters had followed their parents in working for the Goods, the name that preceded Mirro. Nearly 15% of employees, over 430, had served 25 years or more and there were many more approaching this milestone, and many looking forward to retirement. This was to become one of the major factors in just a few years that changed the complete make up and procedures in the manufacturing division.

Gross sales were up again in 1976 (plus 10%) but earnings were down 25%. (Net income of '75 was $3.4M, in '76 $2.5M.) The main reasons had to do with costs of our primary material, aluminum. Prices had risen to a cost of 48 cents per pound, up 17% in one year! Product mix had also changed to lower margined items. Our financial condition was still strong but we all felt that improvement had to be achieved. The Marketing Division was restructured to include profit center business managers. This concept gave closer management control and accountability for final profit results. In Manufacturing we concentrated much effort in reducing indirect labor costs. The major area had to do with material handling costs. Now that the "pressure pan automation" had proven successful and was in full operation, the engineers were looking at what other production items could be converted to like procedures. One such item was the whistling teakettle. Start to finish production time went from weeks to hours! The major improvement in cost was the reduction of handling and storing component parts before the assembly and packing of the product. How? By the use of conveyors and the relocation of the equipment to a central location. "Automation" was becoming a very familiar and often used word in office and shop arenas.

Big changes were still being planned for the future. At the invitation of one of our suppliers, I received approval for sending several engineers to a manufacturing plant in Italy. This firm had been very successful in automating similar items to ours, becoming very efficient as a leader in their industry. Upon the engineers' return, planning began in earnest for the major automation of all "top-of-the-range" cookware. It wasn't long before we in the manufacturing group saw the potential of reducing the need for a large part of our factory space presently in use!

As I look back on it now, the directors, along with President Ziemer, must have felt confident that the decision to bring in new thinking in regard to the manufacturing division in 1965 was a good move. This can only be a guess on my part, but similar action was taken in the marketing-sales division in 1977. A search was made for a top-level individual to bring in fresh thinking for the future. In April of '77, a 37-year-old up and coming individual with sales/marketing experience from the appliance industry was hired as VP of Marketing-Sales. As happened in 1965, when I entered the organization, I'm sure he was given an indication of what his possible future might hold. In contrast to my entrance, however, large changeovers were to take place in the sales area. With the entrance of the new V. P., Frank Prescott, age 59, was given the title of Vice President and Assistant to President Ziemer who was age 62. It was only logical to prepare for the time of Ziemer's retirement. He and the outside directors rightfully saw the need to strengthen the sales-marketing area where he, Ziemer had excelled in his career. This new person's credentials were very impressive. However all experience was in the heavy appliances field, not cook ware. It was evident he would have a learning curve before being up to his task for the world's largest cookware corporation. He was fortunate to have three very talented individuals, Frank Prescott, Frank Timberlake and Richard Stolz to teach him the ropes and tricks of the trade at Mirro.

Here's a note of interest pertaining to new individuals with whom I had the privilege of working. All new members to the Board of Directors since my appointment were: Dr. Robert Spitzer President, Milwaukee School of Engineering; Mr. Bernie Kubale, Attorney-Partner of Foley & Lardner; Quint Willems, President & CEO of The Larsen Company; T. A. Rader, Chairman of the Board & CEO of Allen-Bradley Company. The longer I was exposed to these fine gentlemen the more I admired them and their knowledge of the free enterprise system. Most of all, these were Christian men with high

IS GOD ON OUR SIDE?

morals and, to make an even deeper impression, they were just plain Joes who made me an equal and made me feel at home at all times.

Along with the new concepts of automation and computer controls, labor negotiations and training programs kept me pleasingly busy. Again we reached agreement with the United Steel workers in July, for a three year contract, extending to July of 1980. This now represented 14 years without a work stoppage which also allowed for annual company growth! The years 1978 and '79 proved to be years of equal pressure, excitement, and challenge. I lost a good friend and golf partner when Uriel Garey died of cancer. It was no surprise, but it was sad to see him slowly lose strength over many months. He was a very sharp and talented financial expert and was a real supporter of mine. The only time we had a small disagreement came when it was proposed to build a small addition to the factory at the Mirro Drive complex---this to facilitate an automation project. When he heard of the proposal, he said, "No more brick and mortar, we have too much now!" He never lived long enough to see that this small addition was to eliminate over one million square feet of old building space. Mr. Jim Berkovitz was named Secretary Treasurer in his place. Jim was a member of the computer project team that developed the Production Control System that had become such a wonderful tool for the company. I had spent many hours with him and his accounting staff. He and family lived close to our home on the north side of town.

Sales volume reached $151.6 million in 1979; more than double what it was the year during which I was fortunate to be a part of this team. We now could realize how important our wonderful labor force was that could support the excellent sales people out in the consumer world! At the loss of U.E.Garey, finance department head, Mr. Ziemer felt it necessary to replace him. Mr. Mike Lynch was hired as Vice President of finance in '79. While we soon became good working partners, there lacked that history of how the company growth had taken place, a result of close teamwork between the three key vice presidents. I remained the last of that three as in late 1979 it was announced that Mr. Frank Prescott was to retire as

CHANGES IN MARKETING/SALES; AUTOMATION THE WORD IN MANUFACTURING ➤

Assistant to the President.

These three years, 1977-79, the manufacturing division was kept busy just planning and working hard to keep pace with the continual growth of the sales division. Complete new lines of heavyweight cook ware had been designed and received well by buyers and consumers throughout the country. We were finding it difficult to locate factory space to keep pace with this growth. More and more attention was devoted to the planning for extension of the automation program covering this large volume of heavy weight cookware, plus maintaining customer service at a high level. It was time to finalize these plans, place a cost of investment, and estimate a return on that investment. With the past several successful plans now running, it was much easier for finance and engineers to complete this justification. These plans were presented to the Board of Directors with welcome support from Mr. Ziemer and other officers. Approval was received to proceed with the transition at a cost of near $8 million. The manufacturing people had major work ahead. They had to schedule, execute, and keep in stock all items to be automated. Added to this, two new projects were instituted.

Project #1 was a major energy conservation item at our Plant #6 rolling mill. It involved our two large 45,000-pound reverberate smelting furnaces where aluminum ingot and scrap was melted before being cast into large slabs for rolling into sheet. These furnaces operate in excess of 1600 degrees F, and at 24 hrs per day. The exhaust gasses were normally expelled to the outside atmosphere. Large stainless steel ductwork was used to divert this high temperature air into a mixing chamber and diluted with outside air to 1,200 degrees. This tempered air was then utilized in pre-heating of scrap in two homogenizing furnaces, two slab preheat furnaces and finally in our boilers to generate steam. This rolling mill of over 300,000 square feet produced close to 100% of all our sheet requirements, from heavy-gauge coil to light-gauge rigid foil.

Project #2 was the introduction of a series of new items and processes which included: Improved Teflon substrate, porcelain exterior coating of aluminum, exterior anodic finishing on cookware, chrome plating of aluminum, plus several new products to be introduced.

President Ziemer was now age 64 and a new CEO would soon be selected. At a directors' meeting, the new sales/marketing person was chosen by the Board. (Per the bylaws this selection was the duty of the outside directors plus the outgoing president.) Mr. Ziemer became chairman. Was I disappointed? Yes! I really felt I could handle the responsibilities and had hoped to someday advance to the top. With the help of three remaining seasoned and knowledgeable friends (Frank Timberlake and Dick Stolz in marketing-sales, Jim Berkovitz in finance), all part of the team that had doubled the growth in the past 14 years, I had felt confident in the future. But that was not to be. On January 1, 1980 the new Chief Operating Officer and Executive Vice President was announced and on January 1, 1981 named president. Soon after his appointment in 1980, he hired two vice presidents to his staff; Peter Jung, VP Sales and Dick Schmidt, VP Marketing. (My friends Frank Timberlake and Dick Stolz ,who both reported directly to VP Prescott in the sales division since my joining the company, were now gone.) That was difficult for me to understand and the reason for it is still unknown to me. However, as I look back, how fortunate I was to be accepted so well by the veteran staff in manufacturing! How well we worked together. By using their talents and years of experience, we made the many improvements which, in turn, made growth of the company possible.

The selection by the outside directors was not a big surprise to me, I could see it coming. It was very evident that Mr. Ziemer felt the need for the continuance of leadership to come from someone with marketing and sales experience and, now that Mr. Prescott would soon be retiring, he apparently felt there was a lack of this leadership among the existing personnel. Again, I would have suggested a different course had he or the board members asked my opinion. The reason for my success was the presence of the experienced staff plus the two old timers I reported to! Their past history gave me the

CHANGES IN MARKETING/SALES; AUTOMATION THE WORD IN MANUFACTURING

proper background to make sound plans from which to execute.

So what else was happening in these five years to top all of my work hours? Again, the letters of Eli can sum it up quite well.

April 9, 1974.

Dick's folks seem very lonesome -- -- seemed ill at ease when he called them in Phoenix. We decided to go and visit them for Easter. We plan to stay about 10 days.

Tom's card yesterday said that he had biked 450 miles so far on their trip from Netherlands to Belgium -- then Southwest through Belgium into the tip of Luxembourg. Then into Germany, to the city of Trier on the Mosel River, up to the Rhine and at writing of this card were in Kohn , Germany, headed for Dusseldorf.

I am so proud of dear husband. Conference state meeting on Saturday, March 30 Dick was awarded the Silver Knight Award from the National Management Association.

Louise tells us she received another raise and a promotion to senior analyst at the bank. Mighty proud of her!

October 10, 1974.

Big news! I gave in -- -- Dick has asked me for over a year -- "would you please get a speed bike"-- -- so you can keep up with me. What could I finally say, when a Sears had a 20% discount on bicycles. So last week, we journeyed the country roads, and discovered the beauty of Manitowoc County. And it was fun!

◄ IS GOD ON OUR SIDE?

December 9, 1974.

Last weekend, we shared the glorious Messiah, presentation at Luther College. That's Christmas! All the hope, joy expressed through God's love in verse, and music. It's a cherished tradition on the college campus. Louise and Lon drove with us -- -- Nancy came in her red Pinto and we talked a blue streak! The girls had reunion with all their past classmates.

May 12, 1975.

Tom sent us an invitation to come celebrate his graduation on May 25. He is so thankful, and so excited about having had 4 years of college; he is the most joyous kid I know -- -- so in love with what he is doing -- -- positive in his decision to go on to the seminary in the fall. PRAISE!

On June 30, Dick and I left for Tennessee. The Alcoa Company flew into Manitowoc, with their private plane, taking us to their large lodge in the Smoky Mountains. If that's what it's like in heaven, I am ready! Food -- lodging -- servants -- recreation -- expertise! We even were able to tour their huge Rolling Mill in Knoxville, Tennessee. That was a real treat, exciting to me, all business to Dick.

September 13, 1976.

This Sunday the 19th there will be a special service of dedication for Tom and classmates at the Seminary Chapel. Dick and I will drive over on Saturday, will spend the weekend with Tom. On Monday we plan to tour and bike the region around the Mississippi River from St. Paul down to La Crosse and up the other side. Anxious to just "soak in" that scenic beauty.

CHANGES IN MARKETING/SALES; AUTOMATION THE WORD IN MANUFACTURING

November 16, 1976.

I finished my Old Testament final exams, was such a fun challenge to fit the puzzle pieces together over a year's study. Now, onward to the New Testament, 1st lessons this week. Tom finishes his 1st quarter this Friday at the seminary -- comes home over the weekend for his 1st vacation that will last until November 30. Nancy gets home late the evening of Wednesday the 24th, Louise and Lon will come for the weekend. We are so lucky. Our family is still so close together.

July 26, 1977.

Nancy and Jim's wedding on the 23rd! It was a blessed day sharing, and pride. Tom and Nancy having always been extremely close-- -- it was so heart thrilling to have him participate in the service with Scripture, and sermon -- -- and with Louise as attendant -- -- there was our family together -- just beautiful!

October 9, 1977.

Dick and I spent one weekend biking the Kettle Morraine area west of Sheboygan, it was thrilling with the beauty of the fall colors.

January 12, 1978

Grandmother Thomsen, age 85, died Thursday the 12 of Jan. 1978 at St Mary's Home in Manitowoc. Private family graveside services we'll be on Monday at Mount Emblem

Cemetery, Elmhurst, Illinois.

February 15, 1978

Tom is engaged! He met Barb last April at the Seminary cafeteria. They plan to be married in mid-August. Tom has one more year at the seminary, then will be "sweating it out" for a call to a church.

February 21, 1978.

In April, we will be attending a Metal Cookware convention at Hilton Head Island, off the southernmost tip of South Carolina. Dick just returned from a great learning experience in San Jose, California -- -- IBM training school.

July 24, 1978.

We are rejoicing, and full of happiness that the Lord led Tom and Barbara to meet -- -- she is a very committed Christian -- -- a most lovely girl. We love her as our own and are so happy she is in our family. The wedding ceremony (July 15), and time spent together, gave us a wonderful opportunity to get better acquainted.

April 11, 1979

On 27 March, Pappy had a stroke in the morning -- -- this past Monday night, the 9th, he died. Today, Pappy and Mom *are celebrating their 61st anniversary in heaven -- -- what a happy thought to lighten heavy hearts. The staffs at the hospital were very attentive to him -- the sisters at St. Mary's came almost every night to visit him.*

May 23, 1979.

<u>*'I can do all things in Him who strengthens me; God will supply all that you need from his glorious resources in Christ Jesus.' (Philippians 4: 13, 19)*</u>

June 21, 1979

Tom was interviewed at Wilmington, Illinois on June 9 & 10th -- -- this week he received a letter of Call from the congregation. Ordination is set for Sunday, July 29 at our church in Manitowoc.

Tomorrow, Dick leaves for a business trip to England. Work at Mirro has been very pressing, lots of meetings -- -- many trips -- -- if he isn't out of town, he's having lunch or dinner with business people -- -- I've been rather on my own.

July 3, 1979

(A very profound writing from a letter by Eli!) <u>*"As we all find -- -- there is no black and white -- and the gray matter gets hard to deal with. The joys get overwhelmed with the impossible -- -- all of life is changing -- sometimes to greater degrees -- -- Praise be that the Lord is changeless and constant and sure; our hope and trust is built on a Solid Rock.*</u>

◄ IS GOD ON OUR SIDE?

> *With that assurance -- we can surge ahead, may be unsure and heavy hearted -- perplexed, weak of knees, but He is our strength, and that we can count on!"*

October 22, 1979.

The autumn colors this year are as the deepest and richest in years! Dick and I biked some of Door County to take in the fall beauty. With his traveling so much it was good to have some time together.

CHAPTER 29

Major Automation completed & the "Beginning of The End?"

1980-83

After working with the new president for the two years prior to his selection to the position, it was becoming very obvious to me that his objectives differed greatly from my vision of the future for Mirro. His background was strong in the financial world. This you had to admire. His outside contacts were strong with much depth in the "Acquisition Arena". In the past, when working with Mr. Ziemer, it was a completely different atmosphere. Frequently when business decisions were to be made and he would ask my opinion, I had to be truthful and say I could not recommend such action. I even mentioned to him once that it seemed like I was always disagreeing with him. He often had told us officers that he did not want "yes" men around him; he wanted us to be open and truthful. That I had taken literally. (I was told by my peers on many occasions that this was questionable; it could backfire someday.) Dealing with the new president was much different. There was little request for my opinion. However he did support me in most all I proposed and encouraged our automation with confidence.

In August of 1981, the new president joined me at meetings with all employees in all plants. We laid out the plans to modernize our housewares manufacturing operations. It centered around our Mirro Drive complex. This is the three plant complex located between Manitowoc and Two Rivers consisting of Plant #5 (Stamping and assembly), Plant #6 (Rolling Mill) and Plant #7 (Shipping-Distribution). Over the next 2 ½ years, plants #1 and #4 in Two Rivers were to be phased out and buildings vacated. Jobs and equipment were then moved either to Mirro Drive or to Plant #2 in Manitowoc. Employees at the Two Rivers plants would, for the most part, keep present assignments but at the new locations.

This move was to modernize housewares manufacturing by changing it from batch-type to in-line production, completely eliminating the need for the wooden crates that were used to store in-process parts. Now products being made would move continuously on conveyors from aluminum coil production and stamping at the rolling mill to the adjacent fabrication plant for coating or polishing. Without interruption, the product would move to the distribution center to be packed and shipped. In-process inventory would be reduced by over 80% and time to produce completed product would shrink from weeks to hours.

The key to success was the help and enthusiastic support of all employees involved! This included the work force as well as the management people. There is no doubt in my mind that since first joining the company, my practice of being in every plant each month, meeting not only with the management but also walking the production lines and talking with the workers, paid dividends. It was an exciting time for me. To see years of planning come to reality was a dream come true, not just for me but for many in the manufacturing division. Much credit goes to the experienced staff that worked with me. They had accepted me and I them---we all learned together. This was quite a contrast to the introduction of new blood brought into the marketing-sales division.

Included in the modernization process was the help of many suppliers. For example, many different sizes and shapes of cookware

MAJOR AUTOMATION COMPLETED & THE "BEGINNING OF THE END?"

items were to be mixed on a moving conveyor into a wash machine. How do you separate them as they are conveyed to their next machine station for further processing? We gained the answer from the conveyor people and used newly developed electronic sensors and mechanical gates. Yes, to succeed it took complete confidence and close collaboration as a team. We had to use past experience to sense if new technology was applicable to our products and processes. Keep in mind we had put our toes in the water with the trial automation of the pressure pans and teakettles some time earlier. It was our trial proving ground that was very successful and helped us to be positively confident that all could be successful.

Another major milestone had occurred in the history of the aluminum company called Mirro. To best explain the next events and direction of this company, I'll do my best to relate the beginnings of Mirro. Some liberty is taken as I seek to recall information from other writings. This multimillion dollar business, known as the world's largest manufacturer of aluminum cooking utensils with more than 3000 employees, had a humble beginning back in 1895. A Mr. Joe Koenig established the Aluminum Mfg. Company of Two Rivers, Wisconsin. It is said that he first saw this new metal called aluminum at the Columbian Exposition at the Chicago World's Fair in 1893. Some years earlier, in1864, Mr. Henry Vits had started his tannery business in Manitowoc and in 1898 converted to also use this new metal to produce various items. The new company was called Manitowoc Novelty Company. A merger took place in 1909 when the Manitowoc and Two Rivers companies merged with a New Jersey aluminum venture to create the "Aluminum Goods Mfg. Company". Novelty items such as combs and trinkets were expanded to the primary production of cookware--- namely pots and pans. The manufacturing-minded Vits family seemed to dominate the leadership role for years till Mr. Ziemer became president. The mass production methods of cooking utensils began in 1913 when the company produced an innovative product called the "double boiler" for the Quaker Oats Company. This alleviated the annoying problem of oatmeal sticking to the pan while cooking.

◄ IS GOD ON OUR SIDE?

During World War 1, canteens, mess kits, and utensils were turned out in great volume. The company set out on large scale building expansion programs in both cities, thus producing two large plants in Two Rivers and two in Manitowoc, plus existing buildings. It appears that the New Jersey firm (now known as Alcoa) was very pleased to use aluminum in this way---so pleased, in fact, that they owned approximately 20% of the local company stock. Not only did the Aluminum Goods produce their own name products, but also contracted with others to make any product designed to use this lightweight material. The facilities were engaged in national defense work and in the 1940's, during World War 2, had many contracts. (Aircraft parts, coffee filters, platters, fuel tanks, meat cans, ammunition cases and radar parts) The company had grown very rapidly in both dollar volume and in physical facilities, requiring more and more of a labor force. It was primarily a "manufacturing" complex, constantly expanding to keep pace with a demand for which it was capable of satisfying.

After the 1940s, demand for home products continued and the sales force also grew, along with sales representatives. Again, growth and diversification required expansion of facilities. From the very beginning, the New Jersey partnership had influence in the manufacturing process. A "Rolling Mill" technology had grown with this blossoming business both in Two Rivers and in Manitowoc. This time the space within the two cities was limited. Thus, a 104-acre site was purchased between the two, this to be used for future building expansion. In August, 1957, the company announced plans to erect a new $12 million rolling mill (Plant #6) and company name-change to MIRRO. Shortly after this, the building of a fabrication plant (Plant #5) followed in 1964 by a large distribution and shipping center (Plant #7). (As a sidelight: The next year a young engineer by the name of Dick Thomsen joined the management force of this rapidly growing company.)

And as I stated earlier; "Another major milestone had been reached. In 1981, it was announced that two long-standing, large plants (those

MAJOR AUTOMATION COMPLETED & THE "BEGINNING OF THE END?"

in Two Rivers) would be closed. These were located in a city that had been one of the birthplaces of this company. Technology with automation was beginning to reduce requirements for both space and manpower. Recall back in 1970 when I was spending those long nights plotting the past trend line and predicting the future 40-year requirements for labor and physical space? I convinced myself that some big important happenings had to take place in the way this company met the demands for growth. It was not possible to continue as we had in the beginning or as in past years. It was really fun and exciting for all of us in the planning group to see that "big important happening" become a reality soon. And it all took place as a result of in-house talent---individuals with dedication to great service and pride in their company!

Another major milestone was in the making---one that was not readily recognized or broadcast for public consumption. Had Mr. Ziemer known what it would eventually lead to, he would have been greatly opposed and disappointed. He was such a strong and devoted person to the well-being of Mirro. It was in his blood and his entire life seemed devoted to its success, not just for himself, stock holders, and customers, but for the sake of history and all its employees. He sold the name of Mirro wherever he went, and praised its traditions, products and people! He was the ultimate salesman, his entire career centered around marketing. When it came to running the business he was intelligent enough to seek advice in his own way. As mentioned earlier, he often asked my opinion on decisions to be made regarding operations or subjects in the area of sales. More often than not we were at odds regarding those plans. I was not the only one. It appeared that others had similar experiences but I believe they seldom expressed their view. If he did not appreciate my opinions then why would he continue to approach me with such questions?

Working for the new president was a completely 180-degree turnabout. I have no recollection of his ever asking me my advice or questioning overall decisions. He appeared to me to be a "loner" with his own objectives and was quite determined to achieve them.

IS GOD ON OUR SIDE?

Strengthening and improving the financial bottom line was foremost. No one can object to that in regard to a business. Profit and a strong balance sheet should always be foremost in the operation of any business if it wishes to grow and be viable in its field. But why do you want to be strong and how do you intend to become strong? That is a crucial question. At the time, acquiring other companies was an often-discussed possibility for Mirro. We had been successful in the takeover of National Metal Coatings (Aluminum House siding) of Oconomowoc, Wisconsin in 1964. This added to the volume of metal sheet to be cast and rolled at the rolling mill. In December, 1971, we entered the pleasure boat business by acquiring the Cruisers, Inc. of Oconto, Wisconsin. Preliminary meetings were held with Aluminum Specialty Co. in Manitowoc in which I had participated. This was an area in which our new president was well versed. This I welcomed. However, there are two parties in an acquisition: One party acquires, the other party is acquired. From the outset of the introduction to our new president, I was concerned about the possibility of mergers; be absolutely sure we continued to be the acquirer and not the acquired! I missed that regular contact with the president in which Mr. Ziemer presented his ideas and asked my opinion on many subjects concerning Mirro's ability to maintain its leadership role.

At first all seemed to point in the direction of Mirro being the party looking to acquire others, thus adding to our potential growth. In the early years of our company, recall that a New Jersey company (Alcoa) was an instrumental partner. Alcoa was not only a large stock holder of Mirro, but it also owned and operated the Ware Ever Company. By law, they were now required to divest of our stock and not have a member on our Board of Directors. Without going into details, this was a door opener for someone to become very influential in the business of Mirro if they were to acquire this large block of our stock. Fortunately, Alcoa dispersed the selling of this stock over many firms as was mentioned before. The thought of being the acquired was squelched temporarily, but there still remained a potential of the reverse.

MAJOR AUTOMATION COMPLETED & THE "BEGINNING OF THE END?"

The year 1981 was very challenging with net sales dropping over 15% and a net income loss. The economy of the country had taken its toll on industry throughout the nation. Home construction as well as Pleasure Boat production was among areas most affected and cookware was no exception. It, too, fell over 15% in net sales. (However, listening to the Mirro old-timers, during times of recession, home cooking tended to increase and the cookware industry would benefit in the long run). In early 1982, our president announced that efforts would be made to sell both the builder products and the marine businesses. The reasoning was to streamline the Company, making it tightly focused on consumer household products. Yes, 1981 was a milestone year in our history and this latest move was an indication of what was to come. I, personally, was saddened by this announcement. I could understand it if we did not have long time experience in the areas of home siding and pleasure boating. For example, Mr. Roy Thompson had been founder of the Thompson Boat Company and was the originator of the fiberglass boat. To me, diversification was an asset which could level out ups and downs due to shifts in lifestyle, interest, weather, economy, you name it! Even in my own life, diversification played a large part in my growth and development. (Engineering, accounting, sales, human relation and negotiations.) Equally important to me, both of these areas consumed large quantities of aluminum sheeting. The rolling mill was one of our best profit makers especially if it could operate 24 hours per day. The melting furnaces could not be shut down every day and allowed to cool, the interior fire bricks would be subject to stress that would shorten their life, plus the cost of fuel to keep them hot was energy wasted. Keep in mind the successful growth in the past, when leadership came from the Vits family, all of them coming up through the manufacturing side of the business but inculcated with the importance of developing sound teamwork between all division: Sales/Marketing- Finance-Manufacturing. The new president had successfully sold his plan to the Board and Mr. Ziemer. As an inside director (an employee) I had no alternative but to support the CEO. Inwardly I was not happy to see this retrenching or to see the direction the company was taking.

Project 567 (the automation project that connected the three plants, #5, #6 & #7) was put into motion starting in mid-1981 and was in full swing in '82. The new building was constructed, machinery moved from Plants #1 and #4 to respective areas in Plant #2 in Manitowoc and to this new structure. Plant #1 was the first to close, then #4 in early 1983. Space vacated by the closing of the two plants was close to one million square feet, the new structure, 60,000 square feet. Savings in cost to manufacture the products were of similar proportions. With the boat plant empty in Manitowoc, the aluminum bake ware items were automated here and "corn poppers" that had been moved to Gillett now returned to the main plant in Manitowoc. All this involved lots of action and it sure kept the manufacturing people busy. By 1983, most all of the automation had been successfully completed. It was now time to reap the benefits.

With the complete changes that had taken place in the finance and sales management areas, the close relations and confidence of the past had now changed. With time, there developed more of a "questioning" or "not too sure" or "what's this about" or "none of your business" attitude between individuals of each department. In manufacturing, we had our hands full just to meet time schedules for all the moves that had to take place in the 567 project. In November of 1982, word was received that a firm in Illinois had acquired an option to purchase approximately 33% of the outstanding Mirro stock! My fear of Mirro being the acquired had now reared its ugly head again! How this happened without the Board of Directors knowing of it still remains a mystery to me. Was it by chance or not? The investment firm of Shufro, Rose, Ehrman apparently held the stock in discretionary accounts for a number of its customers. The shares represented the single largest block of stock in Mirro and surely "someone" at Mirro should have been aware of this potential takeover. (I can only guess who that "someone" could have been; I will let you try to guess as well.)The company with the option was none other than Newell. In early March

MAJOR AUTOMATION COMPLETED & THE "BEGINNING OF THE END?"

of 1983 it was announced that both companies had agreed to the merger, pending approval of stock holders. Mirro would become a wholly-owned subsidiary of Newell, joining a group of other such operations. I couldn't believe it! I was really saddened and not too optimistic for the future. The final merger took place soon after. With it came the announcement that the president of Mirro would be promoted to the corporate office of Newell with a new president appointed at Mirro, that individual coming from the ranks of the Newell group.

Here was another shake up at the top levels of management. I was the only officer left who had seen the company's rapid growth in the past 15 years, and to experience the sincere desire for success and well-being of its employees. Teamwork had been present, coupled with understanding of the history of the company. As it expanded, it had become the leader in the industry. I had to wonder where I may fit into this new management group and what direction it would take. In a matter of days I would soon get a hint as to what may lie ahead for me. My new boss, President Bob Gilbert, asked for a report on the different management levels that existed in the manufacturing division. Instead of a report, I requested a few minutes to explain the condition and its history. His response to that meeting was: "It appears you have trimmed expenses quite well-- any chance you and family would consider a move and a good-sized promotion? Nothing official, but I am just curious." That so called off the cuff question was explored and without long dissertation on my part, was considered as a possibility. Sometime later, again after prayer and not much needed conversation with Eli, my answer to Bob was: "It's time for me to retire. I've had a full and gratifying work life. It's now time for Eli and me to relax, enjoy our wonderful family, do a little traveling and explore our hobbies."

President Bob was, without a doubt, surprised with that. "You can't be serious! We need and want you. At least stay with us here, I'm going to need your help." When I convinced him of my full intent on retirement, he relaxed and began to frankly explain his condition.

He, too, had wanted to do the same just recently. His family had a history of heart failure at a rather young age. There was real concern about his future. (Several years later I heard he died of a heart failure.)

I did agree to remain until my replacement could be finalized. With that, paperwork plus party plans were set in motion with good relations and positive feelings on everyone's part. At the age of 58, soon to be 59, I was well aware of sizable reduction in retirement benefits. This had been well thought through by Eli and me before making our decision. We were conservative, and had always lived within our budget. Eli, having been a financial secretary before marriage, had invested conservatively and wisely. Our house was paid for, children through college, and banks paid off.

I had been so fortunate in the past 15 years. I'd worked with some great people, had been allowed to lay out plans in the area of allotted responsibilities, had these plans approved, and saw them become a reality. The greatest accomplishment was that of seeing workers satisfied to the point of zero work stoppage due to union dissatisfaction throughout that period. They were such good workers and the quality of product was outstanding. While the merger of Mirro with Newell proved to be very beneficial to the stock holders if they reinvested in Newell, it was no less than disastrous for the community and the company workers. It is my opinion that had the leadership of the company not been so dramatically redirected in 1980 and the "take over" by Newell properly anticipated with successful avoidance, Mirro would still today be the leading manufacturer of cookware, and a very profitable diversified producer of consumer products. Even with the contemporary global economic conditions, though the company may have had to make drastic changes, it was in a position to be viable and profitable to standards different from those of Newell. At the time of the takeover in 1980, Mirro was as large as Newell in sales! Mirro could and should have been the acquirer, not the "acquired".

MAJOR AUTOMATION COMPLETED & THE "BEGINNING OF THE END?"

It has been said and even placed in documentaries that the decline in Mirro was due to the closing of three plants, as well as the moving of workers to other facilities (In regard to the automation project.) Actually, the reverse was true! It had made the company stronger, more profitable and had made it much more efficient. It was helping in its new-found growth trend. Customer service was greatly improved. Employee attitude was wonderful and the workforce was the best! The decline was more a result of change in management, attitude, lack of good union relations, and loss of employee confidence in this new management.

My decision to retire was not made quickly or in a moment of dissatisfaction on my part. Having heard and been informed of the history of this takeover firm called Newell; it appeared to me that Mirro's future was in jeopardy. The return on investment in the cookware industry, (this included all, such as Ware Ever, West Bend, Regal Ware, even foreign companies) was quite low in the manufacturing arena. Newell was known to expect a rather high return on assets; it appeared to me that those objectives would not be realistically met soon at Mirro. It would take a long time for those proposed and required changes to be made and realized, if ever. I had absolutely no desire to participate in that type of organization.. The demise of Mirro was not begun with the closing of plants, nor was it the result of work stoppages, unions, or employees; we had excellent relations and the best of workers! I feel it actually began in late 1982 and possibly earlier that year with the divesting of the boat and house siding divisions. I mentioned this possibility to Mr. Ziemer, Chairman of the Board at that time, but he apparently was not that concerned. Why oh why did he or I or others on the board of directors not have knowledge of the large block of Mirro common stock being accumulated by the Firm of Shufro,Rose, Ehrman? (Or did some "ONE" person actually know?) I'll let you try to guess that answer; I have my opinion and will leave it there.

◄ IS GOD ON OUR SIDE?

Lesson #10

It's easy to second guess and with hindsight, easy to project, but let me put forth my analysis of what should have or could have happened. In marketing/sales, Frank Timberlake and Dick Stolz (and their staff) had the knowledge and experience of the last fifteen years of rapid and solid profitable growth in the company. Jim Berkovitz, in the financial area was also on board and capable throughout this same period of 15 years. All three were young and aggressive! Diversification had been acquired through investment and acquisition. Costs of producing all products had been trimmed through automation and reduction of overhead (closing of Plants 1, 4 and 3). This company was ready to be the acquirer and a close knit experienced team was just waiting to make the future promising. But that was not to be. Everything changed beginning on January 1, 1981 when the individuals just mentioned above were replaced. The future proved me right in one area; being the acquired was a disaster for community, workers, and suppliers. But it was not for the Thomsen family, who was guided in such a way, that I could comfortably tell President Bob that I was retiring. I will leave it there. I could "cry" when driving past the 7floor landmark building that once housed the largest employer in the area! Windows are broken and structurally it looks like the remains of a war zone. Very sad! My heart and prayers go out to those wonderful employees who once took so much pride in their work and community.

Lesson #11

Prayer is, has been, and can be the answer to ***real change!***.

CHAPTER 30

Twenty Six Years of Retirement and Still Going!

1983-2010

With the house paid for, the children married, and now Dad free of responsibility, how was it for Mother? Was she ready for retirement? How does the old saying go? "The wife's work is never done." There are still the meals to cook, house to clean, washing to do, letters to write, mending, and babysitting for the grandchildren---On and on the tasks presented themselves. Plus, with Eli, responsibilities at church were dearly loved. Yet retirement was a very welcome change and Eli and I became that much closer.

There were many different fields of enjoyment or exploration in which the two of us participated over the next years. All of them were just a continuation of what we enjoyed earlier but, this time around, we could extend each for a longer duration. We loved biking, skiing, car travel, hiking, foresting and flying. I'll start with the flying first, mainly because that is where I personally was most involved directly following my notice to the Mirro-Newell management that I was leaving their company.

Back to flying at last! I had longed to be back in the air with my own plane ever since I was discharged from the Air Force in 1945. The building of an "Ultra-Light" kit plane was a disaster; it was not a conventional designed aircraft and I realized, after only flying it a few feet off the ground, that you don't teach old dogs new tricks when it comes to flying! Soon after that experience, I decided to build a conventionally designed aircraft. The greatest challenge seemed to be where, what, and how do I select a design and start? There were dozens of plans, kits, and models from which to select.

As mentioned, Eli and I had spent many hours at EAA air shows, both in Florida and Wisconsin. Thanks to individuals who saw fit to teach me a few tricks of building aircraft, I was able to successfully select what a senior person should build! To construct from plans, you literally purchased the raw materials and, with hand tools, began the construction. Time to completion could range from 7 to as long as 17 years! No thanks! The kit version was the true answer for me. If ever I were able to fly from my 40-acre plot where the longest runway would only be 700feet, the craft would, of necessity, have to be of the STOL (Short Take Off & Landing.) design. Two such airplanes were completed and certified for flight. (For certification the government inspector had to examine your work) In my case, the cotter pins that secured the 'castle nuts' were bent in the wrong direction, I had to remove all (over 100) nuts and bend new pins properly. (This required a second visit of the inspector!) Wow, you say, isn't that a bit extravagant and expensive! Not really, a small corporation was established: "Wood Aero Inc." I was President Richard and Eli was my Vice President. We became dealers for the states of

Two-Place Homebuilt Aircraft; each 85HP

Illinois and Wisconsin, representing the company making the kits; we actually sold 30 aircraft. The commission received paid for my two aircraft, plus my expenses to travel and help these 30 customers build their craft.

It was a real pleasure to know that Eli just loved to fly with me. We took short fun flights such as the one to Door County for color change in the fall or to small grass landing strips around Wisconsin. We even took winter flights from our hobby farm after snow skis were mounted! The first unit constructed was what they refer to as "stripped to the bone." The kit was received on 1/13/1986, and completed on 3/28/1987. That's fifteen months in all. The second kit took only eight months and it contained what some would call everything but the kitchen sink! Lots of instruments, electric starter, wheel pants, hydraulic brakes, radio---you get the picture! The first was for fun flying, the second for show. I took it to all the air shows for selling purposes. The fun plane was kept at the farm; the show unit kept at the Manitowoc airport.

80 Acre land, trees, hanger, mill and air-strip!

A friend at the airport let me rent a small place in his large hangar. The wings on my plane could be folded back against the fuselage, or could even be placed on a trailer and towed down the street. This gentleman called one late afternoon and asked if Eli and I would like to take a short flight to Green Bay (less than a 30 minute ride) that evening. The moon was to be near full and the sky, clear as a bell, it would be a beautiful night for flying and the sight of the big city was always delightful! Without hesitation we accepted, saying we would be at the hangar in a few minutes! By the time pre-flight was completed and we had boarded his 4-place craft, the moon was in full splendor. I sat in the copilot seat and Eli in one of the rear seats. I promised she could be copilot on the return.

The night was perfect for flying, and it brought back many memories of my Air Force flying days. I hadn't had this thrill of night flying for decades. The air was as smooth as silk. The steady glow of each farm light, and the tractor and auto lights on the highway sparkled like diamonds! A few stars were beginning to show; the sun had just set in the west with a golden glow. The pilot was headed for a Green Bay (Austin Straubel International) airport. He wanted to try out his new credit card (something new in those days) and fill up the gas tank. After landing and filling up, we took off in a westerly heading on runway 24. Eli was now in the right copilot seat. I leaned back and just soaked up the beauty of the glowing city lights visible below and for miles in every direction!

At 3000 ft., almost south center of Green Bay, we heard a very loud explosion from the engine---then complete silence except for the air flowing past us. We had lost all power, the engine was dead! Ron, our pilot, pushed the nose down to keep up safe air speed. The silence was deafening. We were losing altitude now at a steady rate but we could not turn back. The airport was too far behind for us to return there. What would happen next! By natural pilot instinct, Ron and I both were looking for a safe place to land within the next five minutes at the most! Three thousand feet is not very high up when you're above a large city like Green Bay! The freeway, I-43, on the east side of town, was spotted by both of us. Fortunately after taking off to the west, which was mandatory, Ron had turned in the flight pattern, which had headed us to the east toward the I-43 roadway! But could we glide that far? It was soon evident we could not make it! But then, directly below us we caught sight of highway 172 that ran east and west, the main road that led to I-43.

I can't say enough about Ron's fine flying skills! When the engine went dead he was on the radio immediately, conveying our distress, giving our heading, altitude and relaying our proposed and hoped-for destination as decisions were being made! Cool and collected, and my dear Eli sitting next to him, keeping just as "cool" with a little humor mixed in! Fortunately again there were few autos on the road, Ron selected the southbound turn onto the ramp way leading into I-43. He made a perfect landing on the curved upward sloping road! Within seconds we were surrounded by flashing lights of police cars, ambulances and fire trucks! What excitement as three people disembarked with prayers of thanks on their lips! Needless to say, a few headlines appeared in the papers as well as some evening newscasts. This was a real thrill Eli and I never wanted to repeat, but one that was never forgotten. Who said retirement was dull!

"FORESTING" (And flying) While the 40-acre land plot that was purchased contained about 10acres of near virgin forest, we took on the challenge of planting many more trees of diverse varieties. Through the state forestry program, seedlings (approx. 6-inches in height) could be purchased for pennies each. Over a period of several years, thousands were planted in the mostly sandy soil. Red and white pine, spruce, oak, maple and even black walnut nuts were stamped into the sand! Thanks to dear Eli, I would say at least 95% of the seedlings became beautiful trees. Today, some (mainly pine) are now over 35feet tall! At planting time as well as many days thereafter, Eli would, on her knees, pull up any weeds that dared get close to the seedlings. Plus, with a small watering can, she made sure each little tree received a drink. Again, keep in mind, there were close to 10,000 of these trees.

I mention flying in conjunction with "foresting" for one big reason! To build an airplane, a large enough enclosure was required for final assembly! A hangar was to be built to house the assembly plus house the two crafts after completion. Nights at home were spent at the basement drafting table designing the building, then getting a building permit and getting drawings approved. What about the timber required for construction? No problem, there was lots of lumber in those large trees on the 10-acre section of the land! Thus came the purchase of a "Bell Saw" saw mill! I acquired a monstrous diameter

IS GOD ON OUR SIDE?

Shop, Hanger and Saw Mill!

inserted tooth saw blade, run off the power take-off of the Ford Tractor. A run-out table of 24 feet could cut a log 20" in diameter by 12' in length. A building for this mill was constructed first and later connected to the hangar.

Logging of the trees? Our wonderful friends, the Bohrers, now came to my rescue! I didn't know the least bit about running a chainsaw, let alone felling large trees! As a teen, Egon Bohrer had served as a logger out East! He was so happy to join me in the forest; we had a ball seeing how accurately we could predict just where the victim tree would fall! One large beach tree that had been struck by lightning at its very top was one of our prizes. The stump was close to three feet across. When the local forester was called in to examine it, the rings indicated it to be over 140 years old! He even could point out the black ring that indicated the Peshtigo Fire that had raged this far south! This fire occurred on the same day as the highly publicized Chicago Fire, claiming more victims than that in Illinois! So, not only was an aircraft being constructed, but a building to house same. And new trees were beginning life as the old were being put to use. With all the fun, challenges, muscle stiffness, and smiles, time seemed to fly by. Eli was, again, so patient with me and very supportive.

"MODEL RAILROADING" I can't forget to mention this hobby that began in the 1930's when exposed to it at the Worlds Fair in Chicago. An American Flyer set was a Christmas gift and that grew into an interest that continued to grow. Son Tom and I started in earnest while having the new basement added to the house on North 12th street. This was a 10ft x 20ft room that soon became filled with HO scale rails with lots of engines and rolling stock. Of course there were added hills, trees, buildings, on and on!

Hear The Whistles Blowing!

PEDDLING FOR FUN! Bicycling has always been a frequent pastime and means of good transportation in this family! The tandem was in demand on a regular basis! However, Jim and Nancy deserve a lot of credit for the addiction Eli and I shared for biking. Jim was an expert in what constituted a "fine" cycle. To our delight, he made sure that we had fine lightweight 6- or 10-speed bikes! Eli was frequently ahead of me as we peddled most of the recommended and charted Wisconsin routes. One summer, the two of us biked a round trip from Manitowoc, Wisconsin to the tip of Door County. It was an average of 60 miles per day! We did the Elroy-Sparta trail at least four times and the Algoma to Door twice. We so enjoyed our time together and it was very healthful! On one trip alone---the old rail line

IS GOD ON OUR SIDE?

Pockets filled- Ready to Ride On!

near Algoma--- we stopped every mile or two to feast on a handful of wild blackberries. Delicious! Yes, until we looked into our near-empty hands after several stops. We spotted little fresh meat worms, unnoticed in our haste to consume the tasty treats! I'm sure, over the years, we biked every paved road in Door County; the county maps made it easy to mark and record the routes; I wish I had saved those maps and could count the miles traveled---not just to the north but also to many places in the south. For farm use (I let Eli have the big Road Master and later the Grand Marque), I purchased a cargo van, hauling tools plus our bikes to wherever we desired to explore!

SNOW SKIING! We thank Jim and Nancy for introducing us to this delightful winter activity! They presented us with complete equipment on one of their frequent visits to our house. It didn't take long before the two of us were sold on exploring winter scenes while on the long sticks. We even skied by moonlight! Even while still fully employed, I made the mistake of twisting an ankle, but that didn't stop me from future trips. What refreshing times!

HIKING. Wherever we went, it was always exciting to explore the surrounding territory. We loved to walk together, climb the steps, towers, paths, hills or valleys. The trips taken to other states were mainly for the purpose of walking, climbing, and exploring---always stopping to admire the scenery. The Redwoods of northern California was one of our favorites! Even after moving to the Felician Village (A retirement community), we did a lot of walking and hiking; Chilton, Wisconsin had wonderful nature preserves in which we often hiked and explored caves.

AUTO TRAVEL. We both agreed we had no desire to visit foreign lands! The United States was our land (plus maybe a trip to parts of Canada). Of course most routes included family or friends. Yellowstone at Christmas time, the Canadian Rockies, the big Redwoods of California, Lighthouses of the Pacific Coast from California to Washington, Palm Springs, the Grand Canyon , Texas and Arizona, Route 66 to Illinois, then through Florida and up the Atlantic coast. We even witnessed a hurricane while out east and watched the ocean at it most violent. What a spectacle! We saw it all. While a few trips were on commercial airlines, most were by auto. Eli was a wonderful driver and we shared the "left seat" regularly.

Our 50th Aniversary!

In 1997, we celebrated our 50th wedding anniversary, and the entire family gathered together at Galena, Illinois! That is such a great memory and we had a most wonderful time! Shortly before this, Eli and I had gone to Mayo Clinic for our usual "checkup". Eli was diagnosed with some certainty that she had Alzheimer's. As a result we both made the decision to sell our home and move to the Felician Village here in Manitowoc, Wisconsin. It proved to be a rewarding move for both of us.

The motivation for us to make this kind of move was largely a result of having experienced the final "last years" of both sets of our parents. First Eli's mother and dad, who came to live with us. There is no way we could truthfully sense how they must have felt, leaving their home in Chicago and all their familiar surroundings. They seemed happy, but mother Zapel was in such poor health, that I'm sure she had little feeling for what was taking place. Dad had to be very reluctant to make the move but he had no choice. With my parents, similar conditions existed. Maybe even worse, mother's memory was failing rapidly.

Eli was still of sound mind and able to reason. We both did not want to burden our children with having to take care of us; after all we were still in rather good physical health. The thought of "removing the burden of house baby-sitting" and "being free to travel" seemed

Our Wonderful House; "Up For Sale"

like a welcomed alternative. We knew the wonderful "Sisters" at the Felician Village.; here, independent living facilities were available and a beautiful "nursing home" was there if needed. Upon inquiring of the availability of one of the independent "houses", a three- bedroom unit was made ready ""just for us" according to Sister Claude, the administrator! We discussed it together: telling ourselves; "We are in good health;, we are alert enough to make good decisions. We have so many good friends here in Manitowoc, financially we have no concerns, our church is still close by, and we will have years to become adjusted to the new "surroundings" making the "Village" comfortable and "our real home!" I would not call it an "easy" decision to move but it was one that we both felt was a wise and timely one. As in the past, praying together came naturally---, we looked for an answer, not knowing exactly and with certainty when that should take place; yes a "big step".

How we were finally convinced to join the Felician Village? In past summers we had frequently attended the "Farm Festivals" which took place in different counties each year. It had always been a very large, well sponsored and attended outdoor "show" with hundreds of organizations and companies displaying; equipment, materials, feeds, seeds---, you name it--- for the farm community. Why did we go? Remember, we had a "hobby farm", a tractor, an apple orchard, hundreds of trees planted! Yes, it was a fun day for us to venture out into the open air for the day and see the latest in "land use, preservation, and conservation". Right in the middle of all this "hustle and bustle:", Cows mooing, pigs squealing, a dust ball blowing here and there, diesel fumes abundant, stood a "Very Clean White" tent with two spotless, dressed in White Sisters standing in the opening like "Angles" asking us two tired "Seniors" to come in and have some lemonade. You guessed it-- The Angles were there to invite one and all to visit and become a resident of the Adult Retirement Community called Felician Village! Of course we knew them and they knew us! Relaxing with them was so welcomed after walking for hours throughout the day!

IS GOD ON OUR SIDE?

We were not sure if this was their first year to have a "display" tent at this show; it certainly was not our first time. Was it predestined that we should happen to walk past this "white tent" in this multi-many acre fair grounds at this particular time with these two friendly and well acquainted Sisters standing in the tent entrance! I don't know, but what I do know is that -- Our prayers had been answered; Eli and I looked at each other and told Sister Noel, "We will be over to see Sister Claude tomorrow, we think it's possible we' will "sign up" for that vacant house you have at the Village;, we would like to make it our "home".

We would soon develop new friends. We could move about without concern of leaving the house unattended, housekeeping and maintenance at a minimum. We even sold the "80- acre hobby farm" to a couple in Milwaukee who asked me to "use it and watch over it."

Mayo had predicted ten more years "life span" for "173", they were close to being right. While we had our ups and downs in the years to follow, being with family was our most cherished and rewarding way to spend our "hours'. It was my privilege to see to it that Eli was loved and cared for. I hope I lived up to her most deserving expectations and needs. Little by little she lost those "wanted and needed"

life functions but never her wonderful smile or disposition! Sentences disappeared, and she spoke only one or two words at a time. At night bed time, prayer finished, she would always whisper two words: "Thank you." Those two soft spoken words were more than enough to keep me rewarded! She took care of me for 50 years, the least I could do was take care of her for the last few.

On April 12th, 2006 Eli left this world for a "much better one". The following is a reproduction of the notice developed by the family.

ELEANORE MARIE (ZAPEL) THOMSEN PEACEFULLY LEFT HER EARTHLY HOME AT 1608 S. 18TH, MANITOWOC WI. ON WED, APRIL 12, 2006

"My parents Leone E. Zapel welcomed me into this world on May 7, 1926 in Chicago, IL. Three of us children, brother Russel and sister Georgene Pearson grew up in Chicago area, in a close and Christian home.

Aug. 9th, 1947 Richard and I were married at United Lutheran Church, Oak Park IL. A marriage richly blessed by a loving family of three. Daughters Louise (Lon) Horton (children Becky & James), Nancy (Jim) Neumunster (children Gwendolyn & William) and son Thomas (Barb) Thomsen (children Hans, Chris & Nils). Manitowoc became our hometown in the early 1950's; our second home was First Lutheran Church on N 8th St. where I loved to be a member of an even larger "family". My friends were many and I loved them all; thank you one and all for making my life so full and beautiful".

For those who knew her, you surely remember her ever present smile. Her family always came first, teaching us love, forgiveness, tenderness and compassion; here and there ending with a Bible verse spoken or written. Lifelong activities all centered around her church. Leadership in Cradle Roll, Prayer Chain, Missionary for a Day, Christmas programs, Vacation Bible Study, Snip & Sew and Children's Books. Sunday School was so important as she taught the little ones for over 25 years.

Growing in her faith was important to her as witnessed in her participation in Bethel Bible Studies, LDR, Church circle functions, or new member class orientation. Even with all of this there was time for building and uplifting the total family at the north 12th St. home.

We could go on and on, Girls Scouts, Cub Scouts, hospital visitation, nursing home visits; and what it all says - She was a servant of her Lord and Savior Jesus Christ.

Eli most loved the individual moments rather than large gatherings. In those one on one times love was shared and faith expressed. In accordance to Eli's wishes there will be no memorial service and if you wish, memorials may be given in honor of Eli and to the glory of the God she served all of her life to: 1st Lutheran Church, Manitowoc, WI.

Matthew 5:16 "In the same way, let your light shine before men, that they may see your good deeds and praise your Father in Heaven."

John 3:16 "For God so loved the world that He gave His only Son that whoever believes in Him shall not perish but have everlasting life."

"Will see you there!" Love, ELI

CHAPTER 31

"IS GOD ON OUR SIDE? MY SIDE? YOUR SIDE? THEIR SIDE?"

As I have written this "history" of "173 & 3W" there is one thing that boldly stands out and is extremely evident to me; I had left my greatest "Treasure" to spend much too much time alone; I had been selfish in sharing my being available to meet her needs as she had so graciously supported me over the nearly 60 years together. With that said, would I change anything in total today if I could do it all over again? I don't think so. Why? Because even when we were apart we each did that which we felt was important and was right with our Lord and Savior. Time and time again in the past 20- some years of so called retirement, we reminisced and agreed; we had been and still were blessed beyond expectations. "Why change what was so rewarding and good?" "We had a wonderful family we could really be proud of and that loved us as we loved them-- friends that surrounded us-- active in so many ways that we both could enjoy-- security in well-being!

Was God on our side?
    You Bet He Was!
        Why and When?
            Only when we were
                "ON HIS SIDE"

IS GOD ON OUR SIDE?

I'm sure Eli would agree with me, there were many times, whether when alone or together, when God was not too happy with words, actions or thoughts on our part. We were what the Bible describes as "sinful." "Sinful" as so often described, but, after all, can you show me a "perfect" human anywhere now on this earth? Saying we are a Christian does not make us a perfect person but being a Christian suggests and contains an "expectation" for us to strive for so- called "perfection." That wonderful yet simple recommendation of our "counseling" Pastor advising us: at marriage time, "Pray together each evening." "This will be the one thing that tells you when you are on God's Side and when He is at your side." You know; He really wants to be on the side of all us! He became an earthly human, the same as we are, and took our place so that we only have to believe that "He did this" just so we can someday be "at His side". (See John 3:16). Do we, do you, allow Him or invite Him to be at your side? He really wants to be and He is very available any time! He gave us the "mind" to accept or reject. It's entirely up to us: as a person, as a group, as a society, as a nation, a region, a country, and a world!

When we ask the question using the words with "Our Side" we must be very careful because this can cover a group as listed above. It can be very controversial to say the least! You get the picture! How about "wars"? During World War 2, was He on the United States side or did He side with Germany? There were many Christian people in both countries!! I have but one comment and, with it, will leave this one up to you. For the world as a whole I will use a "prayer" to express my thoughts. It is taken, for the most part from one spoken by a respected person, the Reverend Billy Graham. (I'm sure he would not object to my expressing similar thoughts.) The content so impressed me and it expresses my feeling for the need of prayer in these troubled times in which we now live in.

"Heavenly Father, I come before you today to ask your forgiveness and to seek your direction and guidance. Your Word says, 'Woe to those who call evil good,' but that is what we have done. We have lost our spiritual equilibrium and reversed our values. We have exploited the poor and called it the lottery. We have rewarded laziness and called it welfare. We have killed our unborn and called it choice. We have shot abortionists and called it justifiable. We have neglected to discipline our children and called it building self-esteem. We have abused power and called it politics. We have coveted our neighbor's possessions and called it ambition. We have removed the mention of God and prayer from our schools and said it violated my rights. We have removed God from our Government property, even wanting to remove Him from our "currency"! We have polluted the air with profanity and pornography and called it freedom of expression. We have ridiculed the time-honored values of our forefathers and called it enlightenment. We have allowed the devil (Evil) to join our ranks, eroding our beliefs and called it ecumenical. Search us, Oh God, and know our hearts today: cleanse us from every sin and set us free. Help us, our Churches, countries, nations, groups, societies, but especially "me" to be "On Your Side" each day. Amen!"

This "Book" was first intended to only be a "Life History" for future generations of our family. A strong feeling then came: There was a message to be told to others. The two lives that were joined together in marriage, bound solidly by a suggestion of our pastor in our church---, this simple message and suggestion could well be used by future "Church Leaders", lovers young and old, and particularly married couples beginning lives together! My suggestion: Pray together on a daily basis, the three of you; yes, you two and God!

Keep **"God on and at your side"** by your **"being on and at His side,"**, at least once each day!

With that I say "AMEN" and may God Bless you as richly as He has and did Bless us.

173 & 3W

CHAPTER 32

Commentaries From My Four Pre-Readers & Friends

Rev. Gerald Foley

Thank you for letting me read your life's history. I found it very interesting, not only your family but also that of the Mirro Company and your role in its development. You have done a masterful job of sharing your faith, prayer life and religious values and how all of these impacted your life and that of your family. People can learn much from what you have written.

    Signed: Rev. Gerald Foley

Dr. Rev. Bruce Hanstedt

It's perhaps twenty-five years ago that I interview a number of prominent business executives of the parish I served. I was working toward my doctorate. Dick Thomsen was in his early years of retirement from being Vice President at Mirro Corporation, our county's largest employer. These tape recorded quotes from him:

> "Make the best of it now …… In business life the priority of God, family, job may shift-depending on the time at hand."

IS GOD ON OUR SIDE?

"There are times you have to put the family first. Times you have to put the job first. If I'm home on Sunday noon with the kids, don't tell me I have to go down to a meeting. Forget it, fellow! You can wait till Sunday night or Monday."

"Do the best job you can. Loyalty, appreciation of the workers "(is important to me).

"There are times when gifts can hurt the person you're giving them to. It's difficult to determine. When are you going to really destroy a person? (With the gift)"

(On values as modeled in a friend) "He was honest and fair." "He and I had the same kind of outlook on business: what's good for business is good for the employees, but do it right. Let's get rid of the politics. Let's work as a team."

Above taken from: (Doctoral Dissertation: Bruce Hanstedt theological and Ethical Implications of Luke/Acts for Affluent Christians) (Volume II, 1988; housed at Luther Seminary, St. Paul)

I am very pleased that Dick Thomsen has now expanded the above quotes into a highly relevant book on his involvement in work, family and community *as a Christian seeking God's guidance.* I note that now, two decades after the interview, our churches are starting to focus attention on the living out of faith in work, family and community. This is partially evidenced in the most recent Convocation at Luther Theological Seminary and in current theological periodicals.

The current mix of biblical, theological work must certainly include a studied listening to those acutely familiar with the workplace, those who have attempted to walk the walk. We need to listen to Dick Thomsen's book if we want to be relevant. He and his peers are essential to understanding how one seeks to live out ministry in daily life (i.e., family, work, social relationships).

I have known Dick Thomsen, his wife Eli and their children (Louise, Nancy, Tom) for almost forty years. The interchange has been mainly with Dick and Eli, whom I served as parish pastor for twenty-two years. I encouraged their son, Tom, to pursue his call into ministry. I deeply admire and greatly appreciate this truly wonderful Christian family.

I recommend this book for the honesty and insight of Dick's writing as he ponders God's presence and guidance. For the beauty and psalm like letters that Eli shares. I recommend the book for the key, the secret that is shared concerning prayer. Finally there is a business perspective concerning quality of product, distance and closeness (team-ness) between management and labor, and the connection between corporation and community that needs to be listened to, that needs to be read.

Like Dick Thomsen in relationship to his 'boss', I have not always been in the same camp with Dick. That is to say we have not always agreed! That very reality has made me the richer for knowing him.

I recommend, without reservation, and with great enthusiasm, a careful study of this book. It will be a great help in enabling us to be what we are called to be. To be (as wife Eli would say) "Blessed to be a Blessing!"

Signed: Dr. Rev. Bruce Hanstedt

Richard H. Stolz

A true life story, written in the humble manner of a devout individual who enjoyed a busy life in the industrial world. His God, his wife, his children, his work and his community are interwoven in

IS GOD ON OUR SIDE?

this well-written autobiography.

The author's narration reflects a serious and well-rounded industrial career with numerous firms in many different communities, mainly in northern Wisconsin.

His broad experience should be especially appropriate for the young, aspiring segment of our society about to find a "fit" for them upon graduation, where so much depends on practical application of just-learned skills melded in with attitude and humility.

The book illustrates the need for a strong spiritual connection in career planning and execution. Too often we ignore the need for proper approach to problems and people. It is a good lesson on company politics and dealing with life.

General readers and devotees to autobiography can find great pleasure in this book, as well as local Wisconsin folks who will recognize familiar persons and places.

    Signed: Richard H. Stolz

Mrs. Elaine Wigen

There is so much in this book I could mention (especially meaningful and inspiring to me was the story of Dick's career and his advancement in business - so interesting), but I will concentrate on his wife, Eli, and her faith-filled life.

Dick and Eli was a wonderful Christian couple, who lived their faith together and with others, and I relish the memories I have and the effect they had on my late husband's and my lives.

To me, this book is a beautiful love story - Dick's love for God, his family, his career and above all the story of his life with "dear Eli".

COMMENTARIES FROM MY FOUR PRE-READERS & FRIENDS

Dick captured Eli's spirit by including parts of the many letters she wrote to family members.

I knew Eli for many years - from the time we were young mothers to our "golden" years. Eli truly lived her faith in whatever she did (at home with her family, accompanying Dick on business and pleasure trips and outings, worshipping in her church and being involved in many church activities, with her friends - whoever she was with!) She drew people to her with her humility and her beautiful smile that was always a part of her.

Thank you, Dick, for sharing your and Eli's inspiring lives with us. Truly, God was and is "on your side".

    Signed: Elaine Wigen

CPSIA information can be obtained at www.ICGtesting.com
Printed in the USA
LVOW12s0610271213

366973LV00002B/153/P

9 781432 760380